A VISITOR'S GUIDE TO
UNDERGROUND BRITAIN
Caves · Caverns · Mines · Tunnels · Grottoes

Clapham's Ingleborough Cave, North Yorkshire

A VISITOR'S GUIDE TO
UNDERGROUND BRITAIN
Caves · Caverns · Mines · Tunnels · Grottoes

Richard Fells

With photographs by
Tim Grevatt

Bloomsbury Books
London

To Johnny Way,
who first read me *The Cave*
by Richard Church

First published in Great Britain 1989 by
Webb & Bower (Publishers) Limited
5 Cathedral Close, Exeter, Devon EX1 1EZ
in association with Michael Joseph Limited
27 Wright's Lane, London W8 5TZ

This edition published 1993 by
Bloomsbury Books, an imprint of
The Godfrey Cave Group,
42 Bloomsbury Street, London WC1B 3QJ,
under licence from Webb & Bower Ltd 1992.

Designed by Vic Giolitto

Production by Nick Facer/Rob Kendrew

Text Copyright © 1989 Richard Fells
Illustrations Copyright © 1989 Tim Grevatt

ISBN 1-8547-127-X

Printed and bound in Great Britain by
BPCC Hazells Ltd
Member of BPCC Ltd

CONTENTS

INTRODUCTION

Most of us can remember the first time we saw, heard or read something which seemed to throw a new light upon our world, changed the way we looked at life, or even added a wholly new dimension, a new horizon. In my case it stands out in my mind's eye with pin-sharp clarity. I must have been about seven at the time and recuperating from being deprived of a troublesome appendix at a Welsh hill farm belonging to friends of my parents. One sunny afternoon, tired of playing kindergarten games with the farm children, I decided to set off to find the 'blue lake' I had heard my friends talk about. I must have rambled and scrambled a mile or more along old trackways until I was well into the foothills of Esgair Berfa, when I chanced across the rusting remains of a steep cable tramway.

I loved trains, anything mechanical, and curiosity to see what enthralling mechanisms might be found in the winch-house at the top overcame any thought of danger. So I climbed. The winding gear no longer worked and was an anti-climax; the hole in the side of the mountain was anything but. It was only a short tunnel. I could see broad daylight at the other end and, anyway, I was too young to be afraid. Plodding through the stream of water that was trickling out of the mouth, I hurried through into . . . fairyland. Well, no, it was really only a slate quarry, but it was as close to fairyland as an inquisitive seven-year-old could reasonably expect to get.

To my young eyes it seemed vast and the square-cut sides of Welsh slate, weathered pale blue, disappeared sheer below my feet into unfathomable depths of perfectly still, pastel-blue water. The place was diffused with a blue light reflected from the rectangle of open sky above. In the water were fish, shoals of fish, which I later learned were trout. I remember standing on my narrow ledge shocked to a statue by the awe-inspiring beauty of the place. I felt that I could have walked on the water; fortunately I found an old slate-cutting machine and almost lost my fingers finding out how it worked, and then the moment was gone. I suddenly felt cold and alone and returned briskly to the sheep farm for scones and tea, and explanations.

I went back there later, in the company of adults, but it was not the same; this time it really was just a slate quarry. Yet the thrill of that first visit remained with me as the intrigue for things underground has remained with me. I suppose we are lucky if we experience that enhanced sense of wonder more than a few times in our whole life; the kind of excitement that comes close to experiencing love at first sight. While I cannot guarantee that it will happen to you, I can guarantee that there are things to be found underground that will take your breath away, just as the 'blue lake' did for me years ago.

Perhaps we owe it to our cave-dwelling ancestors that for many people the prospect of underground exploration holds a curious fascination. The very word 'underground' speaks of mystery and intrigue, of the secret and the forbidden, of smugglers' caves, derelict mine shafts, secret passages, even hospitals hidden deep under island hills. But where to find all these caves, caverns, mines, tunnels and grottoes? Which ones are open to the public? Which ones are safe for the uninitiated and which are only for experienced explorers, cavers or potholers? Many excellent illustrated guidebooks are available extolling the visual delights of Britain's ever-changing landscape, the architectural splendours of her cathedrals, grand houses or castles, or the historic treasures enshrined within their ancient walls. But the vast majority of such books generally overlook anything below ground level, however interesting or historical. Whilst most authors enthuse freely about the beauties of the British countryside above the ground, for the most part they solicitously avoid any reference to the likelihood of exciting things to discover beneath their feet. Yet, ironically, many of the more interesting underground sites are situated at or near the very beauty spots such publications so enthusiastically extol.

Whether your interests are limited to mere armchair caving or you find the fascination of the underground world altogether too enticing to resist, this book will enable you to discover a whole new wonderland perhaps you never realized existed; a part of our heritage hitherto neglected by the guidebooks. Here you will also find some of the answers to the kind of obvious questions that inevitably crop up when you venture underground with the family, like: 'How are caves made?' 'Where and when was the first tunnel built under the Thames?' 'Is it possible to get from Gaping Gill into Ingleborough without climbing over the top of Trow Gill?' 'How many miles of passages are there at Monkton Farleigh ammunition dump?' So, if rain-swept summer beaches hold no joy and the eternal spires of the shires have lost their ring, why not visit underground Britain? By producing this book, our aim is to introduce the reader to the shadowy wonderland that exists below ground level, beyond the reach of daylight; to lure those with a sense of adventure down into some of the caves, caverns, mines, tunnels and grottoes that abound beneath their very feet. We hope it will appeal to everyone, from those for whom cave exploration is a wholly absorbing pastime to granny and the kids out touring the countryside of a weekend.

Most of the locations we have chosen are readily accessible by car, coach or public transport. Some, however, are not and in order to visit them you will find it is necessary to forsake the car or public transport and tramp bridle-path and byway, nature trail and towpath. (Map references given refer to OS First Series 1:50,000 maps.) But what better way could there be to sample the ever-changing character of these islands than by exploring on foot? To make planning your trip as convenient and easy as possible each of the entries includes a comprehensive list of key information to enable you to easily locate the particular site you wish to visit. In addition entries have been graded to help you decide which are suitable for you or your party. You will find this invaluable when planning underground visits. It should always be borne in mind that the subterranean world is not as forgiving as the world at the surface; not all holes in the ground are like the great incline shaft of Geevor Tin Mine, white-washed throughout for the Queen's visit! So, when in doubt under no circumstances venture where angels fear to tread. And always remember the golden rule – *never* explore underground alone. Oh, and please, when exploring off the beaten track, do take care to observe the 'country code'. Enjoy yourselves!

THE SOUTH EAST

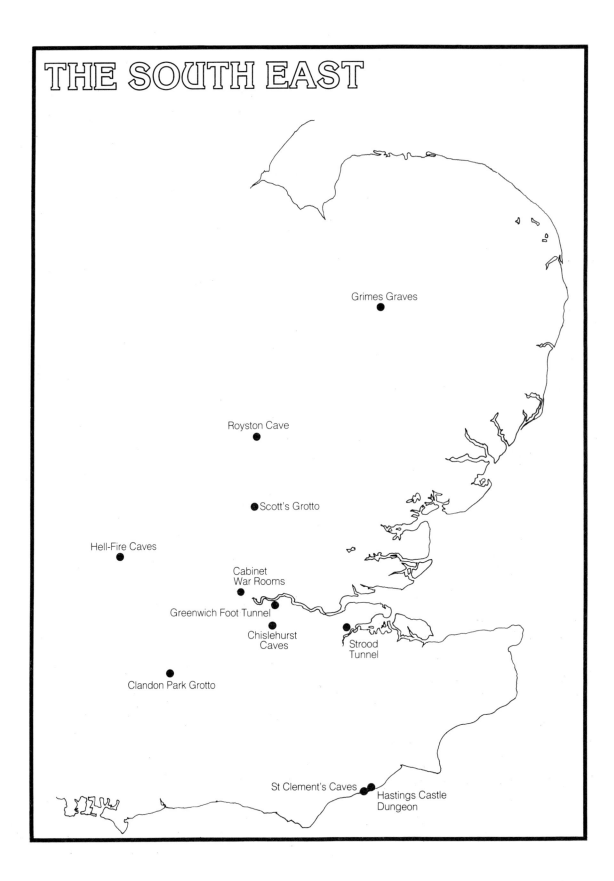

Grimes Graves

Royston Cave

Scott's Grotto

Hell-Fire Caves

Cabinet
War Rooms

Greenwich Foot Tunnel

Chislehurst
Caves

Strood
Tunnel

Clandon Park Grotto

St Clement's Caves

Hastings Castle
Dungeon

The rows of coloured telephones in the Cabinet War Rooms main map room, known to the top brass as the 'Beauty Chorus' (page 14)

Chislehurst Caves: the Roman caves section features some very intriguing wall paintings (page 15)

The patron saint of St Clement's Caves gazing stonily out of his curious candlelit recess (page 23)

One of the six seats in the 'Council Chamber' at Scott's Grotto (page 25)

Although the home counties and the South East do not appear to be particularly well endowed with either caves or mines, there are plenty of unnatural underground attractions to interest the inquisitive enthusiast who hungers after things subterranean. Visual animals all of us, the tendency to only register that something exists if we can see it, touch it or taste it can be something of a handicap in and around London. As we go about our humdrum, day-to-day existence we rarely spare a thought for the labyrinths of underground tunnels, passageways and culverts that honeycomb the ground beneath our feet. How many passengers travelling on the Metropolitan or Circle lines appreciate that they are reliving a piece of transport history every time they journey between King's Cross and Paddington? How many know that during the blitz a total of seventy-nine stations were used as alternative shelters from the German bombs, or that under Whitehall there is a deep-level tunnel linking the basements of all the surrounding edifices of government?

On the subject of tunnels, the pleasant and historic Greenwich Footway Tunnel, with its Edwardian lift and uniformed lift person, makes a refreshing change to the adrenaline-charged, ozoneated atmosphere of the London Underground. Linking the north of the river to the open spaces and outstanding architecture of Greenwich Park it is as good an excuse as any to visit the Maritime Museum, the *Cutty Sark* or even to stand astride the Greenwich Meridian. Another intriguing tunnel is the Strood, on what was once the Thames and Medway Canal. The waterway has since been filled in and now carries trains, not Thames barges, between Chatham and Gravesend.

The most exciting and emotive site in underground London must surely be the Cabinet War Rooms overlooking, or rather underlooking, St. James' Park. It was from this, let it now be revealed, insubstantial 'bunker', that Churchill and his War Cabinet, together with senior military advisers, used all the ingenuity at their disposal to plan, hone and direct the campaigns

which drove Hitler and his advisers into a bunker in Berlin from which he was only destined to emerge one way – feet first.

Whilst the top brass planned retaliatory moves down their 'hole in the ground' it was left to the gallant few to defend the skies against all odds during the late summer of 1940. At the Hendon RAF Museum, surrounded by perhaps the most comprehensive collection of early World War Two aircraft in the world, is a relatively insignificant room with a high-level observation window. An accurate reproduction of the underground Group 11 Operations Room at Uxbridge, better than any film or book, it tells at a glance the story of the momentous hours of the morning of 15th September 1940, remembered today as the turning point of the Battle of Britain. If it had not been for the 'few' possibly none of us would be driving German cars nowadays; we could possibly be making them . . .

On a lighter note, Royston Cave is very much a conundrum wrapped in an enigma. Carved out of the insubstantial Hertfordshire chalk, this bewildering bottle-like 'cave' with its mysterious and somehow discomforting carvings, is like nothing else in earth. The Royston Riddle, it defies the brightest brains to unfathom either its use or its meaning. Very puzzling indeed – if you can fathom out the answer please write.

Grimes Graves, the 4,000-year-old flint mines way over near Thetford, amongst the American air bases, need no explanation. The small but graphically clear visitor centre tells all. This is not the case with the Chislehurst Caves. These are really weird and, of all the places visited, the last one I personally would care to spend the night in alone; perhaps when there were 15,000 other people sheltering from the air raids they might have seemed less spooky. St Clement's in the Hastings cliffs almost come in the same category, some of the carvings are downright disturbing, making anything to be found at Sir Francis Dashwood's infamous Hell-Fire Caves at sleepy West Wycombe seem relatively innocuous.

Cabinet War Rooms

Situated between Downing Street and the Houses of Parliament, the Cabinet War Rooms are the most important surviving part of the underground complex which provided emergency accommodation to protect Winston Churchill, the War Cabinet and the Chiefs of Staff of Britain's armed forces from aerial attack during the Second World War. Concealed under the western end of the recently constructed New Public Offices, this accommodation provided the precedent for the honeycomb of top-secret, underground government facilities which now exist under London, many interlinked by a veritable maze of passages, the full extent of which is still known only to a privileged few.

The reasoning behind the hurried construction of these covert command rooms can be traced back to the First World War and the advent of the bomber. For a century or more, the powers that be had seen to it that wars were fought at a discrete distance, their glorious appetites appeased with cannon fodder; never before had it been possible for an aggressor to threaten the very seat of government back home! Surprisingly, it was not a situation which was given much consideration, until Germany elected to withdraw from the 1933 Geneva Conference on Disarmament, after which the Committee of Imperial Defence began to pay urgent attention to the personal safety of the Government and desk-bound members of the senior defence hierarchy.

Providing adequate accommodation to suit the requirements of security men, typists, secretaries, the BBC, to say nothing of the joint Chiefs of Staff, gave those responsible for masterminding the project many headaches. Nevertheless, rudimentary facilities were ready in time for a disheartened Chamberlain to hold his first and only War Cabinet Meeting below ground five hours after the declaration of war.

By the spring of 1940 the Cabinet War Rooms, as they had by then come to be officially known, were in reasonable working order and able to communicate with the other key centres. The accommodation comprised Cabinet Room, the all-important Map Room, manned night and day throughout the war, an Emergency Conference Room and protected meeting places for the Advanced Headquarters of GHQ, Home Forces (the 'Home Guard'), the Joint Planning Staff and Joint Intelligence Committee, together with combined office and bedroom facilities for the Prime Minister, the Chiefs and Deputy Chiefs of Staff and a typing pool. Space was at such a premium that many secretaries and typists were forced to work from desks in the main corridor. But the inconvenience of being drafted to War Room duties did not end there.

The main criticism War Room inmates levelled at the project concerned the lavatories – or rather the lack of them. Initially they consisted of a row of buckets in the 'Dock'. These were subsequently 'improved' by the provision of chemical toilets positioned near the St. James's park entrance; the arrangement was far from ideal. Perhaps it was partly for this reason that Churchill seldom slept in the basement and a separate suite was commissioned on the ground floor facing the park, known as 'No. 10 Downing Street Annex'. He did, however, make several of his most famous war-time broadcasts from War Room 65A.

Working in such close proximity to the top brass, Churchill's behaviour naturally became the subject for a whole catalogue of anecdotes; in spite of the unpromising prospects prevalent at the time, there was still scope for the ubiquitous British sense of humour to assert itself. An incurable night owl, Churchill frequently worked until past 3.00 a.m., even during the blitz, after which he was wont to take a stroll in the night air or ascend to the roof to glower at the havoc wrought by the German bombers. On one occasion during a particularly heavy raid, the Prime Minister announced his intention to take a walk in the park as soon as things had quietened down. Mr Sawyer, his personal valet, decided enough was enough and with the unanimous backing of his staff, hid his master's boots, refusing to reveal their whereabouts until advised that it was safe to do so. During the winter of 1940, the decision was made to install a new protective 'roof' over the existing War Rooms and beyond. On one occasion the great man was gleefully inspecting the extension of the 'Never-Ending Slab' – a three feet (one metre) thick amalgam of old tramlines and concrete – as it crept inexorably on through the sub-ground floor of the building. Scrambling about amongst the beams he jumped nimbly on to what he thought was hard material and ended up to the shins in wet cement. Apparently his jocund remark to the effect that if he had not extracted himself before the stuff set, the underground Cabinet Room would have had to be repositioned around him, was not universally received with laughter – some of his staff knew his outrageous demands only too well for that.

A visit to these rooms now brings home forcibly the state of affairs prevailing in this country in 1939 and 1940 and gives the term: 'having our backs to the wall' an entirely new meaning. That the rooms have an uncanny quality about them there is no doubt. Disconnected objects stick in the mind: the green baize-lined doors of the Transatlantic Telephone Room; the 'noiseless typewriters' specially imported so that the Prime Minister's correspondence could be typed as he dictated it; a bottle of Pol Roger; the Prime Minister's chamber pot . . .With a little imagination it is not difficult to believe that Churchill has only temporarily vacated Room 65A to pay one last visit to the Map Room next door before emerging for one of his late-night constitutionals. Of all the underground rooms, Room 65 was the most crucial, for here the latest information on all fronts was collected, sifted and summarized for presentation to HM the King, his War Cabinet, Chiefs of Staff, the Joint Planners and the Joint Intelligence Committee. And in the early 1940s the news was rarely other than black. One can almost smell the concerned consultations in the corridor, the prevailing premonitions in the stale air, the odour of disinfectant . . . and, yet transcending the subterranean gloom, could it be possible that there is just the faintest whiff of cigar smoke?

General Information

Owner: Imperial War Museum
Title: The Cabinet War Rooms
Location: Clive Steps, King Charles Street, London
Enquiries: The Curator
Telephone: 01 930 6961
Directions: The entrance is on Horse Guards Road overlooking St James's Park. Underground: Westminster
Access: Open daily all year 10 a.m.–5.30 p.m. including Sundays (closed 1st January, 24–26th December)
Nearest car park: No parking nearby
Time to explore: One hour
Conditions: Dry and air conditioned
Facilities: Museum shop selling a range of relevant publications and souvenirs; lavatories. All facilities are suitable for the handicapped. A lift is available for visitors confined to wheelchairs. Two wheelchairs are available.
Parties: School and coach parties welcome.

Chislehurst Caves

Chislehurst Caves differ from any other cave complex featured in this book in that they are by far the largest system in Britain capable of being explored on foot without special clothing or wet suits. In all there are said to be some 22 miles (35 kilometres) of them, all man-made. They are not, in fact, natural caves, but underground quarries, carved out of the solid chalk by countless human hands. The complex is so extensive that it is almost impossible to grasp their sheer size as they are not laid out in any recognizable geometric form but in random, interconnecting chambers. With a history that goes back to the times of the Druids and beyond, it is hardly surprising that their origins are lost somewhere in the dawn of civilization. It is also not surprising that they are said to be haunted. Several people have attempted to stay alone in the caves all night. All have afterwards stated that they would not care to repeat the

Continued overleaf

experience. One came running out after a mere twenty minutes claiming someone or something was chasing him, but declined to say who or what. Perhaps it was the spectre of the Lady in the Pool, said to have been drowned in the cave by her husband, or of a certain young man who broke into the Caves before they were opened to the public. He was found after about ten days, his fingers worn to bloody stubs through scrabbling around in the dark. Doctors diagnosed death from fright . . .

Utilized as a First World War ammunition dump, Chislehurst Caves saw their finest hour during the Second World War when they literally became 'home' to people from all over London, many of whom preferred a troglodytic existence to the terrors of air raids 'doodle-bugs' and V2 rockets.

Perhaps the best indication of the sheer size of Chislehurst Caves can be deduced from the fact that for something like four years they became the nightly home of upwards of 15,000 persons. The equivalent of ten large ocean liners or forty jumbo jets; the logistics alone of accommodating so many people in a bare cave defy imagination. Even more remarkably, this was no officially organized refuge but the philanthropic gesture of the owner who had first leased the caverns with the intention of starting a mushroom farm.

One of the founder members of the community, a girl of nine, describing her initial impressions of the early days of the shelter, said that her memory was one of terror mixed with excitement. Not altogether surprising, as, in the early days of the venture, there was no electricity nor indeed much in the way of conveniences of any sort; candles and torches were the sole means of illuminating the eerie miles of convoluted corridors and gas masks as well as ghosts were constant companions. Until the Government became interested and bunks were supplied, people slept on makeshift beds on the floor, huddled around their thermos flasks.

The arrival of electric light and bunks transformed the place. Adults were charged one penny a night, children being admitted free. Pitches were allocated and numbered. A Cave Committee was formed and rules laid down. Section marshals were elected and in no time there was a hospital, a church, a library, two canteens, a dance hall, gymnasium, a theatre and a variety of organizations including a children's concert party. How children managed to find their way around the vast, echoing maze was a mystery to the adults, but they did, at least there are no records of any being lost for good! Indeed the project was so successful that the caves became the largest and most important Air Raid Shelter in Great Britain, forcing the Southern Railway to put notices at stations up the line proclaiming: 'The caves are full'.

Being a cave dweller no doubt left its mark on many, especially those harassed mothers with large families who elected to journey across London to the sanctuary offered by Chislehurst, but it seems that few complained. Those who return from time to time speak of a pervading atmosphere of warm friendliness and cheerful communal cooperation. A product of shared hardship? Undoubtedly. Nevertheless, despite the distasteful chemical lavatories, the over-crowding, the over-excited youngsters and the submarine-like confinement, there must have been worse places to spend the long war-time nights. Now all that is a memory and Chislehurst's famous caves have been returned to their ghosts. One cannot help wondering what they must have thought when their space was invaded by hordes of over-night evacuees who drank strong tea and discussed the Second Front in subdued voices, danced or played cards, while over-excited children laughed and cried and scampered through the man-made fastness, shouting 'boo!' at the spooks and playing hide and seek amongst the shadows. Perhaps they enjoyed the company because, curiously enough, while the ghosts rarely show themselves to visitors these days, I am told that if you are very, very quiet and listen very, very hard, you can still hear the sounds of children playing . . .

General Information

Owner: Kent Mushrooms Ltd
Title: Chislehurst Caves
Location: Old Hill, Chislehurst, Kent
Enquiries: The Manager, Chislehurst Caves
Telephone: 01 467 3264
Directions: By road take the A222 to Chislehurst railway bridge. Turn into Station Road then turn right and right again into Caveside Close near the Bickley Arms. By rail from Charing Cross
Access: Open daily Easter to 30th September 11 a.m.–5 p.m., October to Easter open Saturdays and Sundays only, 11 a.m.– 5 p.m. School holidays: Open daily including Boxing

Day and New Year's Day
Nearest car park: Ample free car/coach parking on site
Distance: 55 yards (50 metres)
Time to explore: One hour minimum. Two-hour long tour on Sundays and Bank Holidays
Conditions: Dry graded chalk floors throughout. The caves are easily negotiated by wheelchair.
Facilities: At present there is only a small gift shop and snack bar with picnic tables on site but it is planned to build restaurant, café, gift shop and toilet facilities.
Parties: School and coach parties welcome. Group and evening tours by arrangement.

Clandon Park Grotto

Clandon Park is an outstandingly unusual example of an eighteenth-century English classical country mansion. The house was built on the site of an Elizabethan property purchased by Sir Richard Onslow, a descendant of a politically inclined Shropshire family, whose grandfather had been appointed Speaker of the House of Commons during the reign of 'Bloody Mary'. Known as the 'Black Speaker' on account of his complexion, he was the first of three Onslows to enjoy this position. In about 1731 his great-grandson Thomas, the second Lord Onslow, commissioned Giacomo Leoni to build him a new house in the Palladian manner, a form of architecture made popular by Inigo Jones who had introduced the style from Italy the previous century. Leoni's interpretation of the works of Palladio was, to say the least, unorthodox. Externally, Clandon's subtle scale is dramatized by elevations of red brick contrasted with white stone, a feature which is repeated internally in the form of a magnificent Marble Hall of exactly cubic proportions.

The gardens too have undergone considerable change since the property first came into Onslow hands. The splendour of the original formal setting of the new house was irrevocably lost during the late 1770s when the layout was completely redesigned by Capability Brown in accordance with the informal fashion of the times. But there were gains and it is to this period that the whimsical grotto belongs. Situated opposite the South Front of the house, it forms an interesting focal point of the garden. Close examination indicates that it was evidently built almost entirely from materials which were conveniently to hand at the time of its construction – predominantly brick, flint and a type of ironstone. There are even parts of old wine bottles let into the fabric. Within the grotto itself there are various niches that presumably once contained statuettes but are now regrettably bare of ornament. A splendid sunken bath, complete with steps down to the water, graces the rear of the grotto, suggesting that it once served as a discrete bathing place.

General Information

Owner: The National Trust
Title: Clandon Park Grotto
Location: Clandon Park, West Clandon, Guildford, Surrey
Enquiries: Administrator, Clandon Park
Telephone: 0483 222482
Directions: 3 miles (4.8 kilometres) east of Guildford on the A247 at West Clandon
Access: Open daily (except Thursdays and Fridays) 16th April to October 1.30 p.m.–5.30 p.m. Bank Holiday Monday and the preceding Sunday 11 a.m.–5.30 p.m.
Nearest car park: Ample car/coach parking on site
Distance: 110 yards (100 metres)
Time to explore: One hour
Conditions: Dry
Facilities: Licensed restaurant; picnic area and toilet facilities, National Trust Shop. Picnicking is not allowed in the garden.
Parties: School and coach parties welcome.

Greenwich Foot Tunnel

If anyone knows how many tunnels pass under the Thames, they are not saying. But a glance at a road plan and a map of the London Underground will be sufficient to show that between Chelsea and Gravesend there are three major road tunnels besides the old Blackwall, seven used by the Underground including the BR Waterloo and City and the disused King William Street Line and two pedestrian passageways. Add to these the Battersea District Heating Main, the two deep level Royal Mail links from Colombo House to Trafalgar Square Post Office and Faraday House, Greathead's Tower Subway, the Deptford and Barking cable subways and last but not least the new Thames Barrier service tunnels, and a model of the river sub-strata begins to look like a bad attack of deathwatch beetle.

Although there had already been two unsuccessful ventures to tunnel under the Thames, it was really the Marc Brunel and Son 'Great Bore' at Wapping that started the mania off, albeit somewhat ignominiously. Ahead of its time, a perennial Brunel problem, their cunning travelling shield did the job but was laboriously slow. A series of deaths and inundations did not help and, sadly, when eventually it was commissioned, far from being a success, it quickly became the haunt of Victorian drunkards, muggers and prostitutes.

Wapping's financial fiasco discouraged would-be tunnelers for something like thirty years and then one James Greathead devised an improved version of the Brunel shield. Opened in 1870 and at a fraction of the cost of the Wapping–Rotherhithe, the Tower Subway was completed in under a year compared with Brunel's twenty-six. Enthusiasm returned. With the coming of the 'Tube' tunnels were soon being punched through the London clay as a matter of course to take the noisy new Underground trains. But if peace and quiet is what you are after, there are still two tunnels open only to those on foot at Greenwich and Woolwich.

The Greenwich Footway Tunnel was constructed by the London County Council and opened in August 1902. It provides a pedestrian gateway from Millwall on the north bank of the Thames to Greenwich, one of the most singularly beautiful parts of London south of the river and an area seething with history. With its lining of pale cream glazed tiles the double declivity of the tunnel has utility rather than style, but the neatly domed brick rotundas at either end which house the leisurely wooden lifts and steel spiral staircases are both intriguing and original, as are the lifts themselves. Close by are the famous *Cutty Sark*, that most elegant of all the tea clippers, and *Gipsy Moth IV* the vessel in which Francis Chichester made his single-handed circumnavigation of the globe in 1966 and 1967. Both vessels have been preserved in dry dock and are open to the public at specified times.

Facing the embankment is the Royal Naval College and the Seaman's Hospital and on the other side of Romney Road is the National Maritime Museum and Greenwich Park. The park contains The Queen's House, perhaps one of the most perfect pieces of English architecture in existence. Behind the Queen's House on the crest of the rise is the Greenwich Observatory, home of the Greenwich Meridian – Longitude Zero.

General Information

Owner: London Borough of Greenwich
Title: Greenwich Foot Tunnel
Location: Links Saunders Island Gardens with Greenwich Church Street
Enquiries: London Borough of Greenwich
Telephone: 01-854-8888
Directions: Close by Greenwich Pier
Access: Open daily all year
Nearest car park: Local on-street parking
Time to explore: Half an hour
Conditions: Dry paved footpaths; spiral staircase
Facilities: Public Lift. Boats to Westminster and Charing Cross from Greenwich Pier. Public lavatories.

Grimes Graves

Fenced in by the pine and fir plantations of Breckland Forest is an open expanse of rough, undulating grassland grazed periodically by sheep, rejoicing in the name of Grimes Graves. The term is a misnomer. 'Grim' is another name for the premier Anglo-Saxon god 'Woden' and the sinister 'Graves' merely means holes or hollows. Woden's Holes would be a far better and more descriptive title and might well have prevented a great deal of confusion down the centuries, as the true significance of the enclosure is far from being immediately obvious. Ideally the site should be viewed from the air, preferably in strong slanting sunlight. Under these conditions Grimes Graves begins to yield up some of its secrets. It can be seen that a large area of the site is pockmarked with an intricate pattern of shallow craters, like some disused practice bombing range. Although only a few hundred are still clearly visible, there are thought to be upwards of 700 of them, each one marking the head of a shaft or shallow pit. But, far from being a legacy left over from the last war, these curious craters are all of forty centuries old, for Grimes Graves is the site of a Late Stone Age flint mine complex.

We must thank the late Canon Greenwell for being the first to solve the puzzle of Grimes Graves. Bent on getting to the bottom of this particular archeological conundrum, in the 1870s he spent three years excavating the pit that now bears his name and in so doing laid to rest for ever all other theories as to the origins of the 'Graves', both plausible and otherwise. More recent excavations have shown that the indentation Canon Greenwell chose to investigate was typical of one of the many so called 'deep' shafts. There are also a great many 'shallow' pits, but these are naturally of considerably less interest.

The deep shafts so far excavated have been found to vary from about 32 to 45 feet (10 to 14 metres) in depth and between 13 and 26 feet (4 and 8 metres) in diameter. At the bottom of the shaft there are generally half-a-dozen low galleries just big enough to crawl through, radiating like the legs of a star-fish and linking up with the galleries of adjoining deep pits. Flint comes in various grades; some flints are hard and black and make excellent tools, while others are grey and crack all too easily. The purpose of the deep galleries was to get at the 'floorstone', a particularly good quality of flint found in the hard chalk, or wallstone, deposits which occur at some little depth. Floorstone nodules are to be found only in a limited area in the south-west of the county; the site was therefore one of considerable local importance. Once the flint had been raised to ground level it was dressed into a variety of tools from axes to knives and scrapers for working wood, bone and leather and for doing the thousand and one other jobs needed on a contemporary Neolithic farm.

No one knows whether the tools were used purely by the local inhabitants, or if they were traded farther afield, but at its peak of production, possibly about 2000 BC, Grimes Graves must have been a veritable hive of industry. As all the pits are full of waste material, it appears the system the flint-stoners operated evolved into an organized sequence: digging down to the level of the floorstone, removing the flint over as wide an area as they dared, consistent with not bringing the roof down on top of them, then back-filling with the spoil removed from the next hole. It is intriguing to think that, 4,000 years before Tornados and B52 bombers rent the quiet with their unearthly din, while crouching knappers shaped flint tools for farmers, teams of industrious miners were labouring away underground with nothing more effective than the tines of deer antler picks to chip away the chalk in the limey gloom of Woden's Holes.

General Information

Owner: English Heritage
Title: Grimes Graves
Location: Lyndford, Thetford, Norfolk. Map reference OS sheet 144 TL818898

Continued overleaf

Enquiries: The Custodian, Grimes Graves or Area Custodian, English Heritage, East Anglia Office, 24 Brooklands Avenue, Cambridge
Telephone: 0842 810656 or 0223 462608
Directions: Proceed north-west up the A134 from Thetford for about 5 miles (8 kilometres). Turn left onto B1108 and after about half a mile (0.8 kilometres) turn left again and take the field track to Grimes Graves car park
Access: Open 15th March to 15th October, Monday to Saturday 9.30 a.m.–6.30 p.m., Sunday 2 p.m.–6.30 p.m. 16th October to 14th March, Monday to Saturday 9.30 a.m.–4 p.m., Sunday 2 p.m.–4 p.m.
Nearest car park: Free car/coach parking on site
Distance: 55 yards (50 metres)

Time to explore: One hour minimum
Conditions: Mainly dry. Access via a very steep 32 feet (10 metre) ladder. Hard hats are provided. Grimes Graves are unsuitable for those not able-bodied. Access for the disabled to exhibition area and grounds only
Facilities: There is a small gift shop selling a range of relevant publications, postcards and souvenirs. There are no food or toilet facilities. At a distance of one mile (1.6 kilometres) from Grimes Graves there is a Forestry Commission picnic site with toilet facilities operated during the summer months only
Parties: School and coach parties welcome. Visitor Centre exhibition with displays showing Neolithic flint mining and flint tool production. There is a flint and bone handling collection for use by schools.

Hastings Castle Dungeon

It was no accident that William Duke of Normandy chose Hastings as a base when he invaded England in 1066. The construction of a secure strategic stronghold from which to direct his campaign naturally held high priority in his scheme of things. The resourceful Duke therefore ordered that a series of prefabricated wooden stockades should be made up in sections and shipped across the Channel as part of his armada, so that as soon as his troops had obtained a firm foothold, they could quickly convert the nearest suitable hill top into a fortress. And where better to site a fort and lookout than on West Hill cliffs? A few months later, having achieved his ambition and been safely crowned at Westminister, he had the timber curtain wall replaced with stone and Hastings thus became the first Norman castle to be built on British soil.

For a century and a half the castle enjoyed considerable spiritual as well as temporal importance. A collegiate church was established in the precincts, but far from preaching sanctimony, it seems that the monks of the faculty were noted for their broad-minded benevolence. Hastings was the main point of embarkation for Normandy and the Norman hierarchy were more renowned for their pageantry than their abstemiousness. Things looked good for Hastings – until King John lost his nerve and had Hastings Castle fortifications dismantled, fearful that the assertive Louis of France might take it into his head to emulate his conquering predecessor. Restored by Henry III, the castle enjoyed a second short period of pomp and circumstance. Then fate again took a hand. As if in retribution for the town's past sins, a series of storms of unprecedented violence washed away first the harbour, then a large part of the cliff, causing the entire castle keep to fall into the sea.

Now the castle is a ruin, but a spectacular example of Norman fortified architecture none the less, offering as it does, unparalleled views of the Old Town, the new town and St. Leonards. The so-called 'dungeons' are situated inside the Mount. Access to the two main chambers can be obtained by descending two separate flights of steps. While no one can say with any certainty whether they were used as stores, monks' retreats or prison cells, they do bear a striking resemblance to the dungeons at Pevensey Castle. Whatever their intended use, their most intriguing claim to fame is that they are an excellent example of that rare acoustic phenomenon known as a whispering gallery, although whether by design or accident, is anyone's guess.

General Information

Owner: Hastings Borough Council
Title: Hastings Castle Dungeon
Location: Castle Hill, West Hill, Hastings, Sussex
Enquiries: Hastings Tourism and Leisure
Telephone: 04024 722022
Directions: Near West Hill Cliff Railway
Access: Open daily 15th March to 29th October 10 a.m.–5 p.m.

Nearest car park: Large public car park at the foot of the cliff railway
Distance: 110 yards (100 metres) from the top of the cliff railway
Time to explore: 45 minutes

Conditions: Dry; steep steps. The dungeons are unsuitable for the disabled
Facilities: Cliff top café; lavatories. Castle ruins and cliff-top walks. Audio-visual presentation
Parties: School and coach parties welcome.

Hell-Fire Caves

With its quaint gabled and thatched roofs, West Wycombe, now owned virtually in its entirety by the National Trust, is close to being a text-book Christmas card village. All it needs is snow, the odd robin and a few cheerfully ragged children gazing wistfully at the London stage, to take the visitor back to the century before Dickens; to a time when the village squirearchy was the backbone of the country, when humbug was a mortal sin and being elegantly outrageous was considered infinitely preferable to polite insincerity; to the days when rumbustious drinking clubs and coffee-house politics reigned supreme, before originality became a vice and mediocrity a political virtue. Then, on a bright sunny afternoon, the glittering golden ball atop the ultra-modern church of St. Lawrence would no doubt have proved just as much of a distraction to those wending their way from High Wycombe as it does today.

The difference would have been that few people, locals excepted, would have known that beneath West Wycombe Hill, once the site of an Ancient British camp, there were secret caves penetrating the chalk, rumoured to link both church and the curiously macabre mausoleum crowning the top. And it would have been more than their retention was worth for any local to have dared reveal that their amiable but eccentric squire, Lord le Despencer, was wont to repair to that very dome and carouse away the passing hours in the company of a couple of close friends, quaffing milk punch and admiring the latest additions to his sumptuous romantic gardens, the predominant features of which were laid out in the form of a naked woman! And he a venerable politician and pillar of society? Tut, tut.

But then, where Sir Francis Dashwood, sec-

ond Baronet, later to be branded as 'Hell-Fire Francis' was involved, nothing was ever quite what it seemed.

Born in 1708, young Frank was one of those mortals on whom fortune, in the broadest sense, smiled from an early age. Having succeeded to the baronetcy at the tender age of sixteen, he completed his education by making the obligatory Grand Tour, as befitting one of his status and artistic inclination, in the company of a humourless and over-zealous tutor. On reaching Italy, the 'tour' became somewhat prolonged and it was there that his distaste for the more superstitious practices of the Church of Rome began to come to light.

On the Continent, where the term Holy Day was still tainted with the stench of burnt human flesh, there was plenty of religious hypocrisy. Francis's contempt for anything smacking of sanctimony first asserted itself in Rome during Holy Week. Intrigued, so the story goes, by the scourging sessions that were taking place in the Sistine Chapel, Francis, suitably disguised and armed with a horse-whip, crept inside. Waiting until lights were dimmed and the faithful penitents had begun to half-heartedly flagellate themselves, he manifested himself amongst the congregation, cracking his lash like a latter day lupercalian, convincing many that it was none other than El Diavolo in person. On another occasion he impersonated an aging cardinal, solemnly intoning licentious anti-papist songs, much to the general hilarity of his friends, with whom he appears to have enjoyed a certain popular notoriety. He evidently appealed strongly to the ladies too; amongst his many conquests he was apparently able to list the seduction of the Tzarina Anne while on a visit to Russia.

There seems to be no doubt that the future

Continued overleaf

Lord le Despencer was an extravagant Georgian prankster, a self-confident showman and a rake of the first order, but that was only one side of his character. Charming, intelligent, cultured and a tolerant humanist, he was a man upon whom his peers evidently thought greatness deserved to be thrust. Twenty years a Member of Parliament, appointed Lord Lieutenant of Buckingham, CO of the Buckinghamshire Militia, Chancellor of the Exchequer, and finally Postmaster-General, is not a track record to be sneezed at. A lover of the arts, he was a founder member of the Dilettanti Society. Following a tour of the Ottoman Empire, his next club was named, somewhat tongue in cheek, the Divan. This was followed by the Lincoln, a club formed to enjoy such healthy pursuits as tea parties and bowls. But it was the secret society 'The Knights of St. Francis of Wycombe' that so scandalized polite circles.

For the greater part of its life, from the 1740s until 1763 or thereabouts, the Hell-Fire Club, as it later came to be called by its detractors, met at the nearby Medmenham Abbey on the Thames, where the members, in the guise of monks, indulged in profane revels and sexual frolics in the company of sundry 'nuns'. While it seems unlikely that the club was anything more than an excuse for eating, drinking and being uproariously merry, over the years malicious gossip, inflamed by puritanical prejudice and salacious supposition, exaggerated the activities out of all proportion. After Medmenham's cover was blown following an ugly dispute between members, those remaining faithful to Sir Francis are said to have resorted to the Caves of Wycombe, there to continue their ceremonies in private. There is, however, little to support this theory, although it is possible that after their completion in 1754 certain

'Knights' availed themselves of the caves' privacy in order to indulge in amorous pursuits spiced with a few 'sinfully' irreligious rites, purely for a laugh. Unfortunately, puritanical Victorian dissenters, incensed by the ungodliness they determined to see at every turn, stripped the interior of all evidence, assuming there ever was any, in the mid-eighteenth century. They even vandalized the church and mausoleum in their self-righteous ire. With the exception of a few ambiguous letters, there are apparently no conclusive records of anything untoward. So, to this day, no one really knows what prompted a future peer of the realm to excavate the Wycombe Caves; was it a mere whim or were there other, more disquieting reasons that drove him? Was it plain philanthropy or a Georgian grotto that became a grotto too far? The answer remains a riddle as convoluted as the tunnels themselves.

General Information

Owner: Sir Francis Dashwood
Title: West Wycombe Caves
Location: West Wycombe, Buckinghamshire
Enquiries: West Wycombe Park Office, West Wycombe, Buckinghamshire
Telephone: 0494 24411
Directions: From High Wycombe take the A40 to West Wycombe and the caves are below the church
Access: Caves: open daily March to October, 11 a.m.–6 p.m. and Saturdays and Sundays only November to February, 1 p.m.–5 p.m. West Wycombe House: open daily except Fridays, June to August 2 p.m.–5.30 p.m.
Nearest car park: Ample free car/coach parking at Chorley Road Garden Centre
Distance: 440 yards (400 metres)
Time to explore: Caves: half an hour; house: one hour minimum
Conditions: Dry graded shingle footpaths throughout
Facilities: Small café and gift shop selling snacks, confectionery, soft-drinks and light refreshments; lavatories. The caves are suitable for the disabled. The house is unsuitable for wheelchairs
Parties: School parties and coach parties welcome.

Royston Cave

The history of Royston Cave resembles a riddle to which the answer is another riddle. In August 1742 some workmen, busy making improvements to part of the Butter Market near the ancient crossing of Icknield Way and Ermine Street, happened upon a millstone which, on being turned up, uncovered a long-forgotten shaft which led to a cave. Shaped like a bottle-well, the main cavity was found to be half full of debris which was greedily removed in the hope that there might be treasure. Nothing was found, only some funny old wall carvings in the chalk. No doubt the excavators were suitably disappointed; not so their antiquarian contemporaries who came to take a look. Conflicting theories as to the origin of the cave abounded and as the experts dug metaphorically deeper, so the riddle became more opaque.

The cave itself is an approximately bell-shaped chamber, not far short of 32 feet (10 metres) high; the maximum diameter being almost 23 feet (7 metres). The shape is not absolutely regular, but the variations are minor and the general consensus of informed opinion is that the whole thing is man-made. Around the edge of the floor is a raised step which was at one time octagonal. Similar steps are common in round churches with Templar connotations, such as Temple Church, London, and Holy Sepulchre, Cambridge, giving rise to the theory that the cave was once a Templar store of some sort. Certainly the conditions in the chamber are fairly constant; the ambient humidity is high and the temperature remains a steady 50 degrees Fahrenheit (10 degrees Centigrade). It is thought that this factor accounts for the fine state of preservation of the carvings. As to the carvings themselves, as yet no one has come up with a meaning or a purpose that satisfies all the questions their curiosity inspires.

In essense the riddle might seem simple. The underground room was either a hermitage or a place of storage, and someone with time on their hands and a propensity for whittling away at the chalk, carved a few figures in their idle moments. Some of the figures do look remarkably like doodles, yet others look like the figures seen on medieval brasses. Some of the subjects are obvious such as the Crucifixion and St Christopher, others more obscure. Who would carve from choice the hideously martyred Saints Laurence and Katherine? And what is the significance of the doves and the hearts? Did the high level niches support floor beams or were they for holding lights? No one can say for sure. Was the sculptor one of the two Ladies Roisia, one or both of whom gave their name to Royston – Roisia's Town, a hermit, a crusader or one of the wealthy Knights Templar, as some have suggested? The carvings, having stood the test of time, are still with us and, thanks to the care shown by the owners and their custodians, should remain so, traffic vibration permitting.

General Information

Owner: Royston Town Council
Title: Royston Cave
Location: Melbourn Street, Royston, Hertfordshire
Enquiries: The Town Clerk, Royston Town Council
Telephone: 0763 245484
Directions: The cave is situated in St Catherine's Yard close by Royston Cross
Access: Open under the auspices of Royston District Local History Society from Easter to September 2.30 p.m.–5 p.m. Saturdays, Sundays and Bank Holiday Monday only, or by prior arrangement
Nearest car park: Local Authority car/coach park
Distance: 275 yards (250 metres)
Time to explore: Half an hour
Conditions: Dry with very steep inclined tunnel. The cave is unsuitable for the disabled
Facilities: None
Parties: School parties and coach parties welcome by prior arrangement. Please note that the cave is only large enough to admit ten or twelve at any one time.

St Clement's Caves

The caves have an interesting and chequered history. Burrowing deep into the fine pale sandstone of the cliffs, despite their rambling, apparently random plan, they clearly give the appearance of owing their present form more to man than nature. The most likely explanation for this seems to be that they were originally formed by the gradual erosion of water over a considerable period of time and subsequently modified to suit the eccentric whims of humans relatively recently. But why?

One suggestion is that the almost pure white

Continued overleaf

sand, so soft that it is quite useless for building purposes, may have been used in the local glass industry; some of it may have even been exported to the continent for the same purpose. The most popular and fondly believed theory is of course that the caves were used by the local smugglers. Since Hastings was renowned as a major haunt of eighteenth-century 'free traders', this possibility cannot be discarded. Additional credence is lent by the fact that before a certain John Scott 'rediscovered' the caves in the early 1820s while constructing a niche in the cliffs in which to sit and read, a popular pastime in those halcyon days before television, there had been only one single cave, said to have been of 'no great extent'.

Its actual size at the time is a subject for conjecture, but we do know that it had been bricked up in 1811 by the then owner as the only way of ensuring the permanent eviction of various unsavoury characters who frequented the place. Scott, who evidently enjoyed dancing as well as reading, had a ballroom constructed, still used today for parties and dances. But there is no record of his having excavated a second cave at a lower level. Yet a local reporter visiting the cave in 1826 confirmed that a concealed trap door in the floor gave access to a flight of steps and a lower cave of some length. Could it have been a secret store for contraband? More than likely.

The following year the caves were opened to the public by one Joseph Golding. Over the next few years Golding modified and developed the complex extensively, doing away with the flight of steps by connecting the two caves with a dog's leg tunnel and carving out the elaborate 45 yard (42 metre) long Monk's Walk, seen at its best by candle-light. He also carved the large figure of Napoleon I, now reincarnated as Dr Syn. He then died from consumption, or could it have been silicosis?

There are several other carvings in the cave, some of which are also by Golding. Three, however, predate his hand and one of these,

said to be the St Clement of 'oranges and lemons' fame, lends his name to the caves. Many visitors remark that this section has a distinctly eerie atmosphere. Perhaps it is the sharp contrast to the hustle and bustle of the busy sea-side town outside, but there is something about the quality of deep silence there that some find distinctly unsettling, as if the pale, silent sandstone figures with their attendant sacred urn somehow know more than they are telling.

Most of the other bas-reliefs and graffiti date from the Second World War, during which the caves were used as an Air Raid Shelter capable of sleeping 600 souls. The most important of these bas-reliefs depicts Montgomery, carved by Brian Adnam with a pocket knife, Churchill, arrayed as a Knight of the Garter, and Bunk Harffey, doyen of the Hastings fishing community and one-time secretary of the exclusive Hastings Winkle Club. The carving shows him in characteristic pose, challenging a fellow member by holding up his winkle in the exuberant hope the unseen victim will be unable to respond, and therefore have to pay the regulation fine to the club's Charity Fund for the serious crime of being caught napping with not a single winkle on his person.

General Information

Owner: Hastings Borough Council
Title: St Clement's Caves
Location: Croft Road, Hastings, Sussex
Enquiries: Hastings Tourism and Leisure
Telephone: 0424 722022
Directions: The caves are signposted from the top of the cliff railway
Access: Open daily 17th March to 29th October, 10 a.m.–6 p.m.
Nearest car park: Large public car park at the foot of the cliff railway. It is best to use this and ascend by means of the cliff railway. The caves are then a short stroll from the top station with splendid views over the town of Hastings and beyond
Distance: 440 yards (400 metres) from top of cliff railway
Time to explore: Half an hour
Conditions: Dry concrete footpaths throughout. There is a short flight of steps at the entrance
Facilities: Gift shop; lavatories. The facilities are suitable for the more adventurous disabled. Visitor Centre exhibition containing an impressive collection of smuggling artefacts
Parties: School and coach parties welcome by arrangement.

Scott's Grotto

John Scott was born in Bermondsey in 1730. The son of a Quaker who moved to Ware and made his fortune in the malting trade, he was something of a philanthropist. A Wig, a poet, a keen gardener and a close friend of Samuel Johnson, he was keenly interested in politics, believing that lack of education, not class, made men unequal, stating that 'ignorance is a misfortune, not a crime . . .' What motivated Scott to build his grotto is a mystery. Various suggestions have been made: that it was used for occult practices, that it was a temple to Freemasonry. Neither possibility seems likely. John Scott was a devout Quaker all his life and the Freemasons did not establish a lodge in the area until forty-six years after his death. A far more likely reason was that he longed for some '. . . secret shady cool recess . . .' in which to write his poetry and that grottoes were very much in vogue in the mid-eighteenth century.

Whatever the reason, the result was exquisite, attracting visitors from far and near to Amwell House. Even the redoubtable Dr Johnson, who said that a grotto is a very pleasant place – for a toad, found himself sufficiently beguiled by its subtleties to call it a 'Fairy Hall'. Today, appropriately enough, Amwell House is part of the local College of Further Education; the grotto an all-but-forgotten gem hidden behind an unprepossessing perimeter fence. Originally a grassy sward, religiously mown, led up to a classical miniature portico which huddled at the foot of a leafy knoll crowned in turn by a splendid belvedere.

The lawn is gone, lost when the construction of Scott's Road changed the immediate topography of the site. The Summer House still remains, albeit sadly neglected and overgrown, but both the portico and the vestibule to the triumvirate of passages leading into the grotto, were demolished when the modern dwellings were built alongside. Now the entrance is secreted at the foot of a pretty little wooded dell, squeezed between 1960s housing, its presence as unexpected as it is delightful.

The major part of the grotto, its six remaining chambers interconnected by narrow insinuating passages and light-shafts, is still very much as Scott would have known it. The passageways, lined with knapped flints, lead to small chambers with inexplicable names: Consultation Room, Committee Room, Robing Room. Each is a *tour de force* of shell and flint work in its own right. Most are equipped with niches which at one time boasted wooden seats. The most extravagant of these cells is known as the Council Chamber. The largest enclosure by far, approaching 13 feet (4 metres) in diameter, it is richly decorated with complex patterns of shells, has a multicoloured pebble floor, two entrances, six niches and an elevated domed roof. Conch shells were provided as candle-holders and the curved walls act as a miniature whispering gallery. There are plans afoot to restore the porch and provide a new vestibule large enough to mount a small display setting out the history of the place. It is to be hoped that these come to fruition, as while it would be impossible to restore the setting to its former glory, Scott's fairy-tale grotto certainly deserves a more prestigious entrance than the sombre wooden doors which currently protect its intimate charms.

General Information

Owner: East Hertfordshire District Council
Title: Scott's Grotto
Location: Scott's Road, Ware, Hertfordshire
Enquiries: The Curator, Mrs. Janet Watson, or the Leisure Services Officer, The Castle, Hertford
Telephone: 0920 4131 or 0279 55261
Directions: The grotto is situated about two-thirds of the way up Scott's Road on the right-hand-side behind a wooden fence
Access: Open the last Saturday of the month from April to September, 2 p.m.–4.30 p.m. or by appointment with the Curator
Nearest car park: None. Park in Scott's Road
Distance: 22 yards (20 metres)
Time to explore: Half an hour
Conditions: Dry but too narrow for wheelchairs. Visitors are advised to take extra care in the grotto as the walls are extremely abrasive
Facilities: None. Visitors are requested to bring a torch
Parties: School parties and coach parties welcome by prior arrangement.

Strood Tunnel

Originally conceived as a short-cut for sailing barges operating between the docks of London and Chatham, the Thames and Medway Canal provided a safe alternative for small vessels wishing to avoid the long and frequently choppy passage around the Isle of Grain. The original plan was to make a simple cutting but, on the recommendation of consulting engineers, it was decided to burrow through the chalk. When the project was completed in 1824 for the sum of £250,000, at a length of 2 miles 440 yards (3,622 metres) it boasted the second longest canal tunnel in Britain and the largest, with a bore and headroom of some 26 feet (8 metres).

Its prodigious length, however, exacerbated by the fact that the waterway was tidal, gave rise on busy days to frequent traffic-jams, and, in 1830, a passing place was excavated where the chalk roof was at its shallowest, reducing the tunnel into two lengths of 1,531 yards (1,400 metres) and 2,329 yards (2,130 metres) respectively, separated by a 50 yard (46 metre) opening to the sky. But worse was to follow. In 1844 the company became the Gravesend & Rochester Railway & Canal Company. As with many another canal, this was a development which inevitably spelt doom to navigation. Initially the canal remained open, the single-track railway being built partially on the tow-path, partially on a brick pier staging. But when the company was bought up by the South Eastern Railway in 1846, the waterway was filled in and a second track installed, the line being opened as a double track in 1849.

The most comfortable way of viewing the tunnel is to take the train from Gravesend. Passing through Higham towards Strood, the shorter length is reached soon after leaving Higham Station. There is then a short, memorable glimpse of daylight followed by the second, longer section, after which the railway abandons the line of the old cut, veering off to the right and the Medway Bridge whereas the canal proceeds to its watery destination with the river at Frindsbury Basin, the original terminus of the canal where it joined the Medway.

General Information

Owner: British Railways
Title: Strood Tunnel
Location: Strood, near Chatham, Kent. Map reference: OS sheet 178 711719
Enquiries: British Rail Strood
Telephone: 0634 717133
Directions: Go to either Strood or Higham Station and board the train to the other destination
Access: Any reasonable time
Nearest car park: Higham or Strood
Distance: 275 yards (250 metres)
Time to explore: Half an hour
Conditions: British Railways
Facilities: None.

THE SOUTH WEST

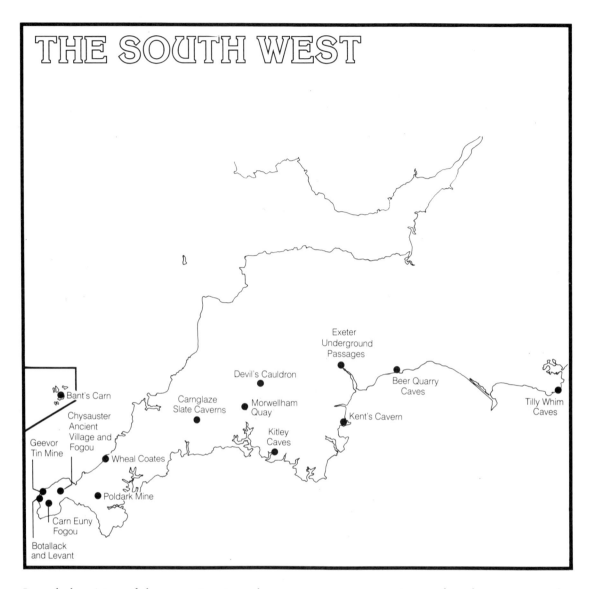

Largely by virtue of the extensive tin and copper mines of Cornwall and Devon, the South West region contains more underground locations than any other part of Britain. From the Bant's Carn, one of three principal Bronze Age burial chambers on St. Mary's, Scilly Isles, to the steep-sided ravine of Lydford Gorge, once the haunt of the dreaded, lawless Gubbins, with its sinister Devil's Cauldron, the South West has much to offer any visitor with an enquiring mind.

In Cornwall particularly, many of the most interesting subterranean sites are unusual in that they are landmarked by the solid granite structures sometimes referred to, erroneously, as 'castles'. These rook-inhabited ruins are in fact old engine houses that date back to the heydays of the Cornish metalliferous mining industry and that great promoter of the Industrial Revolution, the steam engine. Frequently sited over the main pumping shaft of the mine, unless used to drive a 'whim' or a set of 'stamps', you can be reasonably certain that where there is an engine house, the disused mine shaft will not be far away.

Steam has as much to owe the South West as the South West has to owe to steam, for the steam engine was not, as many people think,

Continued overleaf

something that James Watt dreamt up over a cup of tea, nothing could be further from the truth. The first practical steam engine was devised and developed by Thomas Newcomen, engineer, who hailed from the port of Dartmouth in Devon. James Watt merely improved its efficiency by adding a separate condenser and an air pump; that the school-boy myth has been perpetuated for so long simply implies that Watt had a better public relations man than the brilliant Newcomen.

Intriguingly enough, one of the most prosperous mining undertakings in Britain made as much use of water power as of steam. At Devon Great Consols, the mine that supplied the lifeblood to Morwellham Quay, water-wheels were used in place of steam to a great extent.

This did not stop the combine from installing two of the intimidating man-engines, similar to the ill-fated installation that killed so many miners at Levant.

The South West also possesses a good sprinkling of natural caves of which Kent's Cavern is the most widely known. Kitley, situated close to the beautiful River Yealm and the idyllic twin villages of Newton Ferrers and Noss Mayo, despite never having been investigated by the eminent paleontologist Pengelly, is set in surroundings that more than make up for its being less famous. Further east the subterranean stone quarries of Beer, and Tilly Whim are all situated in excellent walking country, so remember to pack the sandwiches and thermos.

Bant's Carn

Bant's Carn is the finest example of the several courtyard house settlements to be found on the Isles of Scilly. Although it originally dates from the late Bronze Age, its main period of habitation was from the second to fourth centuries AD. Adjacent to the site is a field system which still exhibits traces of the characteristic features of the early forms of cultivation, including 'lynchets', the terraces and ridges formed in prehistoric and medieval times by strip ploughing a hillside. An intriguing feature of the settlement is the presence of a fine Scillonian chamber tomb. While this seems to date back to the period of about 2,000 BC, excavations have uncovered pottery from both the Neolithic and Bronze Age. It would thus appear that the grave was in use for a span of at least 500 years. Taking the form of a round cairn with both an inner and outer retaining wall, it measures some 40 feet (12 metres) in diameter and is about 6 feet (1.8 metres) high. The passage itself is approximately 17 feet (5.2 metres) long, lined with courses of dry stonework and roofed with large capstones, one of which has become dislodged. When the site was excavated many years ago piles of cremated bones were found.

The walk from Telegraph Tower via the signposted trail is extraordinarily picturesque and in good weather made all the more unforgettable by the views towards Bryher, the twin hummocks of Samson, the treacherous Western Rocks and the distant Bishop Rock with its well known lighthouse. After paying a visit to Bant's Carn the visitor could be forgiven for concluding that the Bronze Age settlers who first established a farming community there did so as much with an eye for the idyllic visual amenities of the site as for its agricultural possibilities.

Bant's Carn tomb is one of four similar chambers on St Mary's, all of which are well worth visiting. At Porth Hellick Down there is a group of five chambered tombs of which the main chamber is the largest and probably the best preserved on the island. The site is again magnificent, particularly when the heather is in bloom, when the air is filled with the soporific drone of foraging honey bees. The two chambers at Innisidgen are both somewhat smaller but again enjoy a delightful position.

General Information

Owner: English Heritage
Title: Bant's Carn, Scillonian chamber tomb and courtyard house settlement

Continued on page 33

The complex system of labyrinths hand-hewn by the Beer freestone miners (page 33)

The famous Crowns and Diagonal Shaft engine houses perched on the cliffs at Botallack. The headgear pinpoints Allan Shaft, once part of Levant Mine, now in the Geevor complex (page 34)

The vast Main Cavern at Carnglaze is notable for its remarkably convoluted veins of quartz (page 35)

The curving passageway leading from the
circular chamber of Carn Euny Fogou (page 34)

Location: St Mary's, Isles of Scilly. Map reference: OS sheet SV 910124 DE
Enquiries: The Custodian, c/o Chysauster Ancient Village, Gulval, Penzance, Cornwall
Telephone: 0736 61889
Directions: Well signposted from Macfarland Downs near Telegraph Tower
Access: Any reasonable time. The information/sales point at Chysauster is open daily, mid-March to mid-October, 9.30 a.m.–6.30 p.m., mid-October to mid-March, 9.30 a.m.–4 p.m., closed Thursday and Friday.
Nearest car park: Best approached on foot
Distance: 2.5 miles (4 kilometres) by coastal path
Time to explore: Half an hour
Conditions: Open unprotected site. Sensible shoes are advised
Facilities: None. Further information can be obtained from the English Heritage kiosk at Chysauster. In season there may well be cream teas available from the café at Telegraph.

Beer Quarry Caves

The search for the perfect local building stone must have preoccupied the minds of Roman stone dressers and monumental masons from the moment they first set foot on British shores. Inspired by the splendours of the highly developed architectural styles back home, the bleak, misty forests, downs and heaths of Iron Age Britain could only have represented a challenge to their skilful hands; a few glorious buildings would also have been good propaganda. But it was not until after their road builders completed the southern terminus of Fosse Way during the autumn of AD 47 that their attention turned to the creamy cliffs of Beer. How the Roman masons must have rejoiced, for it was here they discovered Beer freestone, a unique 13 feet (4 metre) thick seam of crystalline, granular limestone which not only possessed great natural beauty but similar qualities to the finest Roman building stone as well. Soft and easy to carve when newly quarried, but hardening on exposure, its creamy-white colour and smooth texture also made it the ideal material for intricate carving.

The entrance, set in the face of a low limestone cliff, leads straight into the Roman section where countless thousands of pick marks of those long dead quarrymen are still visible after nearly 2,000 years. The first impression is of the sheer size and extent of the workings, like a series of vast interconnecting vaulted-roofed crypts of cream coloured stone supported on massive columns and, as one proceeds further into the complex, the caves appear to get even bigger and more impressive. As the demand for stone grew, the workings were extended far into the hill, with side galleries driven into the rock to east and west.

Over the centuries the fame of hand-hewn Beer freestone spread. Much prized by medieval masons for both religious and secular buildings, Beer stone has been used to construct and embellish such celebrated edifices as the cathedrals of Exeter, Winchester and St Paul's, Westminster Abbey and the Tower of London as well as many churches and stately homes. After almost continuous use since Roman times, Beer stone's demise came in the 1920s when the famous seam of stone was opencast mined elsewhere. At one stage the previous owners, concerned with aspects of safety, even considered sealing the caves for ever by blasting the entrance. Fortunately the present owners were able to save this historic monument to the quarrymen of East Devon who laboured underground with little more than iron bar and saw for nineteen centuries.

General Information

Owners: Beer Quarry Caves Ltd
Title: Beer Quarry Caves
Location: Quarry Lane, Beer, Devon
Enquiries: 8 Clinton Rise, Beer, Seaton, Devon
Telephone: Caves 0279780 282, bookings 0297 20986
Directions: One mile (1.6 kilometres) due west of Beer Village.
Access: Open daily, April to October, 10 a.m.–6 p.m.
Nearest car park: Ample free car/coach parking on site
Distance: 110 yards (100 metres)
Time to explore: One hour guided tour
Conditions: Generally dry, level footpaths throughout cave interior. Access from the car park is via a steep gully which is difficult for wheelchairs to negotiate. The caves are suitable for the more adventurous disabled. Stout footwear is recommended.
Facilities: Light refreshments and souvenirs are obtainable from the Quarryman's Rest kiosk. Lavatories. Small museum.
Parties: School and coach parties welcome. Reduced rates by arrangement.

Botallack and Levant

Time permitting, having explored Geevor (see page 40), it is well worth taking a walk around the section of the Cornwall North Coast Path between Botallack and Pendeen Watch. The St Just mining area is riddled with the workings of once-prosperous tin and copper mines that did not survive the pressures of economic adversity for which the industry is infamous. The undertakings run in an almost unbroken chain from Cape Cornwall to Pendeen Lighthouse. The list reads like the roll-call of Lean's Engine Reporter. There was Boswedden, Kenidjack, Wheal Owles, tragically flooded in 1893, Wheal Edward and further east the most famous of all, Botallack. Here there are numerous ruins of engine houses, several chimneys and a labyrinth once used to produce industrial arsenic. Close by the new headgear astride the Allan Shaft are the so-called 'Bunny Adits'. Industrial archeologists are still debating the precise antecedents for these curious burrows, but it is thought that they are amongst the oldest mine workings in Britain and may even date back to the Bronze Age when Cornwall was the centre of the known world's tin trade. At the picturesque Crowns engine house can be found the diagonal shaft down which the Duke and Duchess of Cornwall (later Edward VII and Queen Alexandria) descended in 1865, a mere two years after a link broke in the iron hoisting chain, sending nine miners to their deaths.

Further east still are the ruins of the celebrated old Levant which lasted longer than most, only to succumb to economic strangulation, never having recovered from the man-engine disaster of 1919 in which a total of thirty-one lives were lost. A small engine house on the cliffs contains the Levant whim engine, the oldest beam winding engine of its kind in Cornwall. Now in the care of the National Trust it can be viewed by arrangement with Geevor Museum. Boscaswell Downs main shafts are situated in the centre of Pendeen village, but all that is left to mark the undersea levels of Pendeen Consols is a ruined count house.

General Information

Owner: West Penwith Council
Title: Botallack and Levant Mine Ruins
Location: Botallack Head Area, Botallack, St Just, Cornwall. Map reference OS sheet 203 362337
Enquiries: Those wishing to visit Levant Engine House should first contact the Geevor Museum
Telephone: 0736 788662
Directions: From Botallack village on B3306 take the unmade road signposted 'Count House Restaurant' and proceed to the cliffs
Access: Any reasonable time
Nearest car park: Ample free car parking above cliffs
Distance: Botallack 110 yards (100 metres), Crowns Engine House 440 yards (400 metres), Levant Engine House 1 mile (1.6 kilometres)
Time to explore: Two hours minimum
Conditions: Open cliff top site. Stout footwear is recommended. Always beware of unfenced shafts and unstable masonry
Facilities: None.

Carn Euny Fogou

When visiting Carn Euny Fogou it is advisable first to go to Chysauster Ancient Village English Heritage kiosk to obtain relevant information. The site, situated on the side of a hill at a height of about 500 feet (150 metres) is approached across farmland but is well signposted. With wonderful views to the south and west right out to the Scilly Isles on a fine day one can see the sea on two horizons. The site was originally discovered by miners prospecting for tin during the first half of the nineteenth century. Intrigued by the atypical layout of the site, between 1863 and 1868 William Borlase carried out excavations which led to the discovery of an extremely fine souterrain or fogou in the centre of a group of four courtyard houses. Remarkably well preserved, having survived pillaging over the centuries, and of its type unique, it is embellished with an unusual circular chamber as an addition to the long and slightly curving passage 66 feet (21 metres) in length.

First surveyed in the nineteenth century, the characteristic courtyard houses of Carn Euny were apparently built in three stages, the earliest of which dates back to the Iron Age, although there is some evidence to suggest that the site may have been settled even prior to this. The second and third phases of building cover a period from about 300 BC to approximately AD 50, by which stage courtyard houses had become a firmly established form of early first millennium architecture. One of the most peaceful places to be found in Cornwall, but for the occasional tractor, the present-day sights and sounds of the area around Carn Euny cannot differ much from those experienced by the original inhabitants of the dwellings over 2,000 years ago.

General Information

Owner: English Heritage
Title: Carn Euny
Location: Sancreed, near Penzance, Cornwall. Map reference OS sheet 203 403288
Enquiries: The Custodian, c/o Chysauster Ancient Village, Gulval, Penzance, Cornwall
Directions: Well signposted from A30 at Lower Drift.
Access: Any reasonable time. The information/sales point at Chysauster is open daily, mid-March to mid-October, Monday to Saturday, 9.30 a.m.–6.30 p.m, Sunday 2 p.m.–6.30 p.m. Mid-October to mid-March closed Thursday and Friday, open Monday, Tuesday, Wednesday and Saturday 9.30 a.m.–4 p.m., Sunday 2 p.m.–4 p.m. (Note: English Heritage opening times are currently under review.)
Nearest car park: Just beyond Brane Farm
Distance: 330 yards (300 metres)
Time to explore: Half an hour
Conditions: Open unprotected site. Sensible shoes are advised.
Facilities: None. Further information can be obtained from the English Heritage kiosk at Chysauster (see page 36).

Carnglaze Slate Caverns

Carnglaze is situated in the valley of the River Loveny, a tributary of the Fowey, on one side of a steep, wooded ravine. It is thought that the 'old men' originally chose the site, over 250 years ago, because the river had exposed beaches and ledges of slate as it forced its way down to the sea. Initially they developed a traditional open-cast quarry, the object of the exercise being to produce high quality roofing slate. Much of the slate removed was either of an inferior standard or lost during splitting and shaping and, after a while, the company were faced with the problem of disposing of the considerable quantities of waste material which were beginning to hinder production. The construction of a massive wall to retain the spoil improved the situation for a while, but eventually the decision was made to mine the slate underground.

Driving under the hill was a radical step to take, but the wisdom of doing so soon became apparent. There was no longer the problem of excavating and disposing of the surface overburden, reducing at a stroke the time spent on non-productive work. The quality of slate improved progressively as the workings went down. An additional incentive was that there was a strong mining tradition in the area with techniques that were readily adaptable to quarrying underground. There was also the local climate to consider; this part of Cornwall experiences over twice the average national rainfall. Working under cover meant that production could continue in all weathers, an important consideration from the employer's point of view.

Before the coming of the railway, made possible by the construction of the Brunel bridge at Saltash in 1859, the slate was transported up country by packhorse train to the ports of Polperro and Looe. With the completion of the Great Western Railway, it became more expedient to despatch the slate by horse and cart to Doublebois Station and send it on by rail. Slate was much in demand in the building boom of the second half of the nineteenth century and as towns like Plymouth doubled their populations, so business flourished.

Continued overleaf

The total extent of the caverns may never be known as so much debris was dumped outside, that the original entrance became obstructed. This process was repeated, necessitating the progressive raising of the means of access which now bears little relationship to earlier layouts. Some idea of the vast amount of slate removed can be got from the sheer size of the chambers. One of the most interesting features of the caves is the way in which natural formations within the rock have been exploited to permit impressive spans of slate to be left unsupported in total safety. This feature can be seen at its best in the Main Chamber and in the reflection of the natural slate roof seen in the crystal-clear, green-blue waters of the famous underground lake.

Eventually competition from quarries closer to the railway made St Neot's inviable and all underground work stopped in 1903. The caverns did, however, have their moment of fame during World War Two, playing a vital part in the war effort which even now cannot be overestimated; they became a major depot for the safe keeping of Royal Navy rum. The vast quantities stored, albeit under ideal conditions, pending distribution, did not impress the numerous colonies of bats, who promptly fled away, apparently unable to tolerate the intoxicating fumes given off by the rum barrels.

General Information

Owner: J Riveria
Title: The Carnglaze Slate Caverns
Location: St Neot, near Liskeard, Cornwall. Map reference OS sheet 201 189667
Enquiries: Mrs T Wilton
Telephone: 0579 20251
Directions: From the A38 (between Bodmin and Liskeard) Carnglaze lies halfway along the road to St Neot.
Access: Open daily from Easter to September 10.30 a.m.–5 p.m.
Nearest car park: Free car/coach parking on site.
Distance: Cars 110 yards (100 metres), coaches 220 yards (200 metres)
Time to explore: 45 minutes
Conditions: Dry footpaths throughout. There is a long flight of steps down to the floor of the caverns.
Facilities: Cavern Gift Shop selling snacks, ices, soft drinks and souvenirs; lavatories; attractive, well-laid-out gardens; conservatory.
Parties: School and coach parties welcome by prior arrangement.

Chysauster Ancient Village and Fogou

Situated in a spectacular hill-top setting and surrounded by an extensive field system, Chysauster is the largest of several similar ancient, stone-walled village sites found on the Land's End peninsular. Thought to have been built during the late Iron Age/Romano-British period, the group consists of a total of nine courtyard dwellings, eight of which are arranged in pairs and in effect form a rudimentary village 'street'. One pair of houses is in such an excellent state of preservation that they only appear to need re-roofing to become habitable. In addition most of the houses have the benefit of a terraced garden plot and almost all still retain such features as drains, paths, paving and the central, socketed, stone base for the main supporting roof post.

Putting a precise date on the construction of Chysauster has proved to be difficult. Despite the fact that a Bronze Age burial cairn has recently been discovered nearby, no houses from this period have so far been unearthed. Pottery found at Chysauster belongs in the main to the second and third century AD. Consequently there is a strong consensus of opinion that courtyard houses belong entirely to the Roman period. The question is, did the Ancient Britons copy the lavish villas of the Roman nobility with their splendid atria or were courtyards a logical development of earlier dwellings? Whatever may be the answer to that conundrum it is believed in any event that Chysauster was abandoned altogether during the third century AD.

Little had been written on the history of these ancient Cornish villages up to the end of the eighteenth century, but local folklore indicates that Chysauster was used by Methodist preachers and became known as the 'Chapels'. In 1873 William Borlase, the noted Cornish archeologist, removed earth and rubble from what is now house number six. Further exploration in 1897 revealed house number four, but it was not until 1928, when a major excavation under the direction of TD Kendrick of the British Museum and Dr Hugh O'Neill Hencken was undertaken, that the full importance of the site became apparent. As a result, the then owner graciously decided to place a large proportion of the site under the guardianship of the Office of Works. In 1931 further excavation revealed a number of other houses and later a fogou.

Originally about 50 feet (15 metres) long, the fogou, situated to the south of the central part of the village, is currently in rather a sorry state of repair with the entrance partly blocked by sand. Basically dating from the early Iron Age, fogous continued to be constructed until after the Roman Occupation. While they are relatively rare, other fogous are known to exist both in Cornwall and Brittany, notably at Carn Euny, Halligue, Pendeen and Lamorna. The precise purpose of these interesting tunnels is a subject on which experts beg to differ.

General Information

Owner: English Heritage
Title: Chysauster Ancient Village
Location: Newmill, Penzance, Cornwall. Map reference OS sheet 203 473350
Enquiries: The Custodian, Chysauster Ancient Village, Gulval, Penzance, Cornwall
Directions: Well signposted from B3311 and at Newmill on the Penzance–Gurnard's Head Road.
Access: The information/sales point at Chysauster is open daily mid-March to mid-October, Monday to Saturday, 9.30 a.m.–6.30 p.m., Sunday 2 p.m.–6.30 p.m. Mid-October to mid-March open Monday, Tuesday, Wednesday and Saturday 9.30 a.m.–4 p.m., Sunday 2 p.m.–4 p.m. (Note: English Heritage opening times are currently under review.)
Nearest car park: Ample free car park near site
Distance: 650 yards (600 metres)
Time to explore: 45 minutes
Conditions: Open unprotected site. Sensible shoes are advised.
Facilities: English Heritage kiosk

Devil's Cauldron

Lydford Gorge lies in a secret valley on the western outskirts of the historic village of Lydford. Bypassed by the main road and abandoned by the railway, Lydford slumbers in quiet tranquility amongst the foothills of north-west Dartmoor. With ruined castle, chapel, church, and inn it seems the perfect place for the traveller to enjoy an unhurried lunch or take an innocent stroll in the hazy moorland sunlight; and indeed it is, but it was not always so. Surprisingly enough this small Devon village has a reputation for fame and infamy quite disproportionate to its size. The Tower of London excepted, there can have been few names in the kingdom capable of striking more terror into the hearts of miscreants than that of Lydford.

The mother parish of Dartmoor, and indeed the most far-flung in England, Lydford was once a market town of some considerable standing. Originally part of a national defence network designed to stop the advance of the marauding Danes, until the thirteenth century it enjoyed considerable military and commercial importance. During the reign of Ethelred the Unready it even boasted of being the site of the Royal Mint. But competition from Okehampton and Tavistock caused a fall-off in trade, the castle fell into disrepair and Lydford must have appeared to be in sorry decline. Then, in the fourteenth century, the tinners of Cornwall fell out with the tinners of Devon and when the latter met at Crockton Tor and elected to retain the old castle keep exclusively as their prison and the seat of the Stannary Court, their decision changed both Lydford's prosperity and its reputation.

In those days the local tin workings yielded large profits. Not only that, but tinners enjoyed a Royal Charter which virtually put them above all legal jurisdiction; in effect they were entitled to dig for tin pretty well anywhere. Understandably this led to differences of opinion and the only recourse was to law – 'Lydford Law'. By the seventeenth century, the 'Law' had become a byword for savage sum-

Continued overleaf

mary justice. Apparently it was common practice to have the execution first, adjourn to the pub and hold the trial – to keep the records straight – afterwards. Penalties for lesser offences were barbaric beyond belief. Whosoever coined the phrase 'T'were better to be stoned and pressed or hanged than spend a night in Lydford Jail' was not joking. Anyone accused of adulterating tin was compelled to drink an appropriate number of spoonfuls of the metal, a punishment that was known to leave a particularly unpleasant taste in the mouth; tin only becomes easy to swallow if heated to well in excess of twice the temperature of boiling water.

While there is nothing to connect the idyllic secret valley of Lydford Gorge with the macabre history of the castle, there is a quality about the Devil's Cauldron that somehow echoes the shuddery reputation of the infamous jail only too closely. The gorge is 1.5 miles (2.5 kilometres) long and has an entrance at either end. The quickest way to the Cauldron is by way of the Main Entrance at the northern (village) end. From the splendid Information Centre a short, steep path leads down beneath a canopy of trees to the banks of the fast-flowing River Lyd which over countless thousands of years has carved the steep-sided valley from the solid rock. The pathway crosses the stream and continues to the head of the gorge. Here the terrain becomes more rugged and the track enters a narrow ravine where the visitor finds on either side, great dripping banks of green lichen and moss hanging from vertical walls of wet rock. A fine mist pervades the entire area, soaking everything in its path as, with a roar that belies its size, a miniature torrent rushes headlong through a series of tortuous cataracts, each proceeding constriction being narrower than the next.

To reach the Cauldron it is necessary to trust in a catwalk of slippery, timber planks. The final section, greasy with spray and shining in the dim light of the chasm, is supported by freely swinging chains. From here, suspended over a mesmerizing whirlpool of insanely turbulent water, those who have not had second

thoughts, and a surprising number of visitors do, may look fleetingly into the very crucible itself. Here one could be forgiven for concluding that the scriptures have got it wrong; there are no fires in Hell, just cascades of tumbling, boiling water. Despite the fact that the ravine is only about 60 feet (18 metres) below the road bridge at this point, the effect is memorable to say the least, even when the flow rate is moderate. But it is when the Lyd is in spate that the Devil's Cauldron comes into its own. At such times it ceases to be an object of curiosity and wonder and, living up to its name, becomes lethally awe-inspiring. For this reason the northernmost end of the gorge is closed during the winter months.

Much of the remainder of the gorge remains open all the year round and is well worth exploring as it is an Area of Outstanding Natural Beauty in the definitive sense of the term. The variation of scenery is quite memorable at any time of the year, but to see it at its best Lydford Gorge should be visited in the spring or autumn. At either time it is a magical place to stroll amidst the peace and quiet of Pixie Glen, past the turmoil of Tunnel Falls, to the splendour of the 90 feet (27 metres) White Lady Waterfall. But to see the natural water-works to best advantage a visit to the gorge shortly after a period of moderately heavy rain is to be recommended.

General Information

Owner: The National Trust
Title: Devil's Cauldron
Location: Lydford Gorge, Lydford, near Okehampton, Devon. Map reference OS sheet 201 502835
Enquiries: The Administrator, The National Trust, The Stables, Lydford Gorge.
Telephone: 082282 441
Directions: At Dartmoor Inn, 3.7 miles (6 kilometres) north of Mary Tavy on the A386 Tavistock–Okehampton road, take the turning for Lydford and proceed through the village.
Access: The gorge is open daily from Easter to October 10.30 a.m.–6 p.m. The Devil's Cauldron is closed during the winter season but the White Lady Waterfall is open daily all the year round, 10.30 a.m.–5 p.m.
Nearest car park: Free car parking on site at both Main and Waterfall entrances
Distance: From Main Entrance to Devil's Cauldron 330 yards (300 metres)
Time to explore: One hour, but allow two hours minimum to explore the whole gorge.

Conditions: Some of the footpaths are steep and narrow and may be slippery in wet weather. Stout footwear is recommended. The gorge is unsuitable for the disabled, the visually handicapped or those suffering from circulatory or respiratory conditions.

Facilities: Manor Farm Tea Rooms; tea hut selling confectionary, soft drinks and light refreshments; picnic areas; lavatories; National Trust Gift Shop.
Parties: School and coach parties are welcome but it is advisable to make group bookings in advance.

Exeter Underground Passages

The passages that weave their way beneath the streets of central Exeter were once part of a unique medieval water system created by the Cathedral during the thirteenth century to ensure a reliable supply of drinking water. In order to achieve this desirable convenience they utilized an existing twelfth-century passageway which already connected St Sidwell's Well with the conduit in Cathedral Close. At a later date the layout was improved and extended to enable water to be brought both from the Cathedral and City wells to the so-called Great Conduit at Carfax. As the city grew in size and importance, so the system was extended to link up with conduits beneath High Street and South Street.

The vaulted roofs of the passages take on a variety of forms. Some sections are simply variations on the common or garden barrel vault, whilst others assume the shape of an irregular pointed arch or a truncated triangular form. In height the passages vary from approximately 3 feet 4 inches (1 metre) to 14 feet 9 inches (4.5 metres) while their width varies from 1 foot 7 inches (0.48 metres) to 3 feet (0.9 metres). For the most part the passages are lined with local red sandstone and breccia although some sections have been constructed purely by hollowing out the natural rock.

Visitors to the Underground Passages are taken on a guided tour along the Cathedral passage, which dates back to 1346, to the junction with the City passage, constructed in 1420, and then on to a section known as the Great Chamber. Part of the original twelfth-century

tunnel from St. Sidwell's Well can also be seen, as can a short section of the Cathedral passage which leads to the Upper Longbrook Valley. This section now terminates in a dead end beneath a grill in the pavement behind Debenham's department store, thought to have been one of the original access points to the system. A loop of the old Cathedral passage actually passes under Boots The Chemist, but as it is both low and narrow it is only accessible to those prepared to proceed at the crouch.

Further sections of tunnel do still exist, but for the most part they are either too low and narrow for easy access or have been blocked or rendered unsafe by the foundations of buildings, drains, water pipes, service ducts and the bombing Exeter suffered during the Second World War.

General Information

Owner: Exeter City Council
Title: Exeter Underground Passages
Location: The Roman Gate, High Street, Exeter, Devon
Enquiries: Administrative Officer, Royal Albert Memorial Museum, Queen Street, Exeter
Telephone: 0392 265858
Directions: The Roman Gate is in the High Street in the centre of Exeter
Access: Open Tuesdays to Saturdays, 2 p.m.–5.15 p.m.
Nearest car park: King William
Distance: 440 yards (400 metres)
Time to explore: Half an hour
Conditions: Dry footpaths throughout. There is a flight of steps down from street level and the roof is low in places. The passages are unsuitable for the severely disabled and for wheelchairs.
Facilities: Interpretation centre
Parties: School parties and coach parties welcome but access is limited to twelve persons at any one time. Book at the RAMM for tours between 10 a.m. and 12.30 p.m.

Geevor Tin Mine

Geevor Tin Mines was founded in 1911 by re-working the old mines of Wheal Stennack and North Levant. In those days the main shaft was the one now situated in the main car park and named after the first chairman of the company, Oliver Wethered. After the end of the First World War, a new hoisting shaft called Victory was sunk to an eventual depth of 1,577 feet (480 metres). As work below ground extended, an old shaft of Boscaswell Downs Mine was re-opened and deepened to 1,350 feet (411 metres) as an access for men and materials and as a means of escape.

The museum contains many mining relics accumulated over the years including old photographs, ore samples, old surveying instruments and a multitude of other fascinating items associated with the industry.

The underground workings now extend for more than 2 square miles (5 square kilometres) around these three shafts and connect up with the old Levant. Worked continuously from 1820 its levels stretched out under the Atlantic for a mile or more and to a depth of 2,100 feet (640 metres) below adit. One of the great tin and copper mines of Cornwall, it suffered a serious setback when the top of the man-engine sheared, precipitating its human cargo to the bottom of Allan's shaft. A section of the failed rod and strap together with a diagram showing details of the ill-fated apparatus is one of the more gruesome exhibits now on view in the museum. The mine nevertheless struggled on, finally succumbing to the strangulation of falling metal prices in 1930.

Below ground the visitor can not only obtain a very real impression of just what conditions must have been like in the old days, for the countless thousands of men who laboured from cock-crow to sunset amidst the granite and killas of south-west Cornwall with only a flickering candle to work by, but find out first-hand what modern hard-rock mining is all about. You will learn about the dramatic plugging of the breach in part of the old Levant, where, working some 220 yards (200 metres) out from the base of the cliffs in 1965, engineers eventually succeeded in making the flooded mine watertight. With the old undersea levels rid of water they were then able to construct an inclined extension to Victory shaft, opened by the Queen in 1982, making it possible to extract tin from beneath the Atlantic Ocean once more. Unfortunately, after so much development work, due to another sharp fall in the world price of tin in 1985, the mine was forced to stop full-scale production. Nevertheless, at the time of writing, the company are permitting conducted tours below ground for visitors to see the workings themselves: a unique opportunity not to be missed.

General Information

Owners: Geevor Tin Mines Plc.
Title: Geevor Tin Mines Museum and Tourist Facility
Location: Geevor Tin Mines Museum, Geevor Tin Mines Plc., Pendeen, Cornwall. Map reference OS sheet 203 376338
Enquiries: The Museum Manager
Telephone: 0736 788662
Directions: Take the A3071 out of Penzance. Proceed for 5 miles (8 kilometres) then take the B3318 to Trewellard. The Geevor Tin Mines Museum is clearly signposted.
Access: Geevor Mine operates a Tourist Amenity which is open daily to the public from Easter to October, 10 a.m.–5 p.m. Guided tours of the treatment works Monday to Friday, 10.30 a.m.–4 p.m. except Bank Holidays.
Nearest car park: Ample free car/coach parking on site
Distance: The Victory Shaft is situated approximately 550 yards (500 metres) from the museum itself.
Time to explore: Allow at least two hours
Conditions: Visitors wishing to go on guided tours of the surface treatment plant and the underground workings must be fully able-bodied. Protective clothing is not essential but stout footwear is recommended. Protective headgear is provided free.
Facilities: Café serving hot and cold meals all day. Gift shop specializing in books on the mining and geology of the area. Above ground is the unique Cornish Mining Museum which houses the Trevithick Collection.
Guided tours of the working surface treatment plant. Guided tours of Geevor Tin Mine subject to availability.
Parties: School and coach parties are welcome but it is essential that groups wishing to take the underground tour should book well in advance.

Lydford's Devil's Cauldron: 'All hope abandon, ye
who enter here' as Dante would say (page 37)

Torquay's famous Kent's Cavern decked out for Christmas awaits the arrival of Santa Claus and his toy-making elves . . . (page 43)

At Kitley Caves only the narrow access-ways break the unexcavated flowstone cavern floor with its giant stalactite columns (page 44)

Kent's Cavern

Situated in a picturesque, quiet, wooded valley within easy walking distance of the centre of Torquay, Kent's Cavern must currently rank as one of the most important British caves open to the public. While rightly famous for housing some of the most beautiful examples of natural underground architecture to be found anywhere in the world, it is perhaps less well known as the cave which effectively established the reputation of William Pengelly, not only as the significant paleontologist of his time, but as the first man to produce tangible evidence supporting Charles Darwin's revolutionary theory of evolution.

William Pengelly, FRS, was born at Looe in 1812, the year the Russians took steps to rid themselves of Napoleon. Largely self-taught, but with a natural abundance of energy for learning, he left his native Looe in the 1830s and set himself up as a teacher in a small day school in Torquay. His interests were broadly based; astronomy, anthropology, meteorology, mathematics, were all subjects he set about mastering. He was also particularly fond of geology, a subject which, in due course, led him to become a founder member of the Torquay Natural History Society. Persistence and application were the hallmark of his character and drove him to examine in depth any subject which interested him. It therefore came as no surprise to his fellow members that when, in 1858, some workmen by chance uncovered a cave in Brixham which had clearly been sealed for thousands of years, it was a challenge Pengelly, with his disciplined, enquiring mind, could not resist.

Obtaining permission from the owner and backed by funds from the Royal Society, he quickly organized a painstakingly punctilious excavation of the debris lying on the cave floor. Hitherto exploration of caves for scientific purposes had been pursued in altogether too piecemeal a manner for the pedantic Pengelly. He insisted that the entire cave deposit consisting of cave earth and flowstone should be removed systematically, layer by layer, so as not to muddle or lose the least scrap of evidence. Strictest checks were kept on the position of each and every object found so that their interrelationship and historical sequence could later be analysed from the records, enabling him to establish the strict stratigraphical order of the finds. Thus he was able to ascertain, not only the different species lying buried in the cave earth, but also the ratios which the numbers of individuals of the different species had to one another and to relate them by their relative position in the deposit to a nominal time scale. By applying his methodology he virtually obviated any possibility of confusion over the order in which the deposits had been laid down. This had never been done before.

After perfecting his method of stratigraphy at Windmill Hill Cave, Brixham, in 1865 Pengelly redirected his energies to the excavation of the stalagmite floor of Kent's cavern. Here, to the profound dismay of contemporary God-fearing Christians, the vast majority of whom firmly believed that Darwin was a dangerous heretic, Pengelly unearthed from the soil of Torquay a pandora's box of animal remains controversial enough to set tongues wagging from the erudite halls of the Royal Society to the cloisters of the Vatican. Those belonging to species still extant, such as lion, hyena, horse, bison, stag and grizzly bear, could be explained away easily enough; at one time the Garden of Eden included Torbay. But the presence of bones and fossils of extinct giants like woolly rhinoceros and mammoth, great cave bear and sabre-tooth tiger, were somewhat more difficult to dismiss in Biblical terms, particularly as they were buried beneath the debris of past millennia. Even more sobering were the human remains, fragments of bone and stone artefacts, lying beside the ashes of cooking fires grown cold perhaps 300 centuries years ago.

Recent research has confirmed that, like Creswell Crags, Kent's Cavern is effectively one of Europe's pre-eminent cave 'time

Continued overleaf

capsules' of ancient history. Using modern techniques it has been possible to re-examine the human artefacts and remains discovered in previous excavations and, amongst other things, date them far more accurately than ever Pengelly was able to do. In 1988, the human jaw bone and teeth discovered in 1927, on being radio-carbon dated at Oxford, proved to be fragments belonging to a 'modern' type of human being who was alive and well and living in Torquay some 31,000 years ago. This exciting discovery identifies Kent's Cavern man as the earliest modern human so far discovered in Europe and represents the first conclusive evidence that Modern man took over from Neanderthal man.

General Information

Owner: Kent's Cavern Ltd
Title: Kent's Cavern
Location: The Caves, Wellswood, Torquay, Devon
Enquiries: The General Manager
Telephone: 0803 24059
Directions: From Torquay harbour take the Babbacombe road to Wellswood after approximately one mile (1.6 kilometres). Proceed 220 yards (200 metres) down Ilsham Road past St Matthias church and the entrance is on the right-hand side.
Access: Open daily 10 a.m.–4.30 p.m.
Nearest car park: Ample free car/coach parking on site
Distance: 55 yards (50 metres)
Time to explore: One hour minimum
Conditions: Smooth, graded footpaths throughout. There is one short flight of steps.
Facilities: Refreshment buffet and outside sun terrace; gift shop selling souvenirs; waiting room; lavatories. The caves are surrounded by well-laid-out grounds; informative exhibition area; special events by arrangement. At Christmas the caves are 'leased' to Father Christmas and his elf toy-makers.
Parties: School and coach parties welcome.

Kitley Caves

Kitley Caves lay undiscovered by man for many thousands of years until local quarrymen accidentally uncovered a cave entrance while blasting for limestone in the early 1800s. Since then the cave system has been opened up, first by a previous owner of the Kitley Estate who was interested in the study of bones and fossils, then a fashionable pastime, and, after his successor resumed quarrying activities, again in more recent times.

The limestone layers, once living coral, were laid down on the bed of the warm seas that washed over much of Britain during the Devonian period, some 400 million years ago. The development of the caves can be traced back to the beginning of the Pleistocene Era of about two million years ago, when acids in the flooding waters of the melting ice masses dissolved out the rock, forming tiny passageways and indentations. As these grew they carried more water which in turn dissolved yet greater volumes of material, thereby enlarging the cavern. As the end of the Ice Age brought about a drop in the rate of flow, so underground rivers deepened the tunnels, cutting scallops out of the rock and forming the characteristic key-hole shape found at Kitley today.

It was at this stage that droplets of water from the roof, depositing minerals on the cave shoulders and floor, formed the spectacular calcitic pillars and massive flowstone pendants hanging from the roof with no visible means of support. Subtly illuminated by concealed electric lighting, these colourful stalagmites (which 'might' one day reach the roof) and stalactites (which grow downwards and hang 'tight' to the limestone ceiling) add dramatically to the visual charm of the caves. But these are not the only items of interest found at Kitley. In the course of numerous excavations on the site, bones and fossil remains have been found in great quantity. Many of these are now on display in the museum which is based entirely on finds made in and around Kitley. The exhibits include the tooth of an elephant and bones of bear, hyena, deer and many small rodents.

The origin of the animal remains has been dated back from the last inter-glacial period right up to the present day; animals still occasionally become trapped and die in the farther reaches of the cave as yet unopened to visitors. The full extent of the system is not yet known but is believed to extend over an area of at least 2 square miles (5 square kilometres), the parts that are accessible and safe for visitors representing but a fraction of the whole complex. Massive boulder chokes made up of thousands of tons of fallen rock make one giant chamber for the moment completely inaccessible, but as there are upwards of three dozen known entrances to the cave complex from Tor Quarry alone it is not outside the bounds of possibility that further reaches of the caves will eventually be opened up to public view. Exploration still continues.

Although it is possible to reach the caves from the village of Yealmpton itself, by far the best approach is by the footpath from the caves car park. This delightful walk closely follows the fast-flowing River Yealm through an enchanting tree-lined valley. In this sylvan setting those with sharp eyes may spot brown and sea trout and other small freshwater fish, water vole, dippers, grey wagtails and the occasional bright flash of a blue kingfisher; if you are very lucky, in season, you might even see salmon running for the reeds further up stream. Bring your camera!

General Information

Owner: Kitley Estate
Title: Kitley Caves
Location: Yealmpton, South Devon. Map reference OS sheet 202 573513
Enquiries: Kitley Estate Manor Office
Telephone: 0752 880202
Directions: From Plymouth proceed towards Yealmpton along the A379 Plymouth to Kingsbridge road. Take the turning for Newton Ferrers (light traffic only). The turning for the car park is at the foot of the hill.
Access: Open daily Good Friday, Easter, and from the Saturday before Spring Bank Holiday to September, 10 a.m.–5.30 p.m.
Nearest car park: Ample car/coach park near site
Distance: 440 yards (400 metres) from the car park
Time to explore: Half an hour. One hour including museum and woodland trail.
Conditions: Generally dry, graded footpaths. The caves are unsuitable for the severely disabled.
Facilities: Gift shop selling a wide selection of mineral samples and fossils, sweets and ice-cream. Lavatories. Museum. Woodland trial. Rough adventure playground with rope suspension bridge over the River Yealm.
Parties: School and coach parties welcome.

Morwellham Quay

Hidden deep in the Tamar Valley in an area officially designated as being of outstanding natural beauty, Morwellham Quay was once the greatest copper port in Queen Victoria's Empire. The history of the port as a centre of the Devon non-ferrous metal mining industry goes back at least 700 years, but the period of Morwellham's greatest wealth and importance was during the nineteenth century. Prior to the construction of railway lines to Plymouth, the Tamar was the easiest and cheapest source of transport. Thanks to a fortunate combination of topography and geology, the adventurers who financed mines like Wheals Friendship and Crowndale were able both to harness the forces of gravity and obviate the out-dated, inefficient and prohibitively expensive pack-horse teams which had hitherto been the sole

means of transporting the heavy copper ore to the Tamar.

The solution, to build a canal, fed by the waters of the Tavy and terminating 237 feet (70 metres) above the Tamar at the head of an inclined plane railway, powered by water from the canal itself, was a stroke of genius. The scheme was not without its drawbacks. Although a mere 4.5 miles (7 kilometres) in length, it was necessary to tunnel 1 mile 780 yards (2 kilometres) through Morwelldown and this took fourteen years. But when the first barge of copper ore emerged from the portals at Morwellham, it began a period of ever increasing prosperity that was to envelope the village and its tidal quayside for sixty years.

By the time the phenomenally profitable Devon Great Consols came on stream in 1848

Continued overleaf

the village was growing in importance by the hour; it is said that at the height of the port's prosperity in the mid-1850s, up to 4,000 tons of copper ore would be awaiting shipment on the quay at any one time.

The mines of the Tamar Valley provided the major portion of Europe's copper. As the quantity of ore extracted grew, so too did little Morwellham. With a dock big enough to take six 300-ton schooners, 4.5 miles (7 kilometres) of railway and a second, steam powered, inclined plane for ore trucks, the bustling village was rapidly becoming a boom town. But locked away on the secluded tidal banks of the Tamar, its prosperity was inextricably bound up with the prosperity of Consols and, when the fortunes of that mining monster began to ebb, Morwellham went into terminal decline. Rich seams of copper had been found in both Australia and America. When the pumps of Devon Great Consols, ailing for a quarter of a century, were finally stopped in 1901 the village was already but a shadow of its former glory.

Effectively the death knell had been rung with the coming of the Tavistock broad-gauge line. This had taken the steam out of the Tavistock Canal as early as 1859 and by 1868 when the George and Charlotte closed the end was inevitable. Gallantly the community struggled on, but before long the giant water-wheels ceased turning, silt stifled the river, weeds defaced the tiled quayside and the once-crowded dockyard with its elevated tramways, stores, workshops and assayer's laboratory fell into disrepair. It was indeed fortunate both for Morwellham and for all who are interested in the past, that the enterprising Dartington Hall Trust came to the rescue. Following an extensive programme of restoration, Morwellham quay has been recreated to become a living museum of nineteenth-century industry and culture. Now it is possible for the visitor to rediscover the inventiveness of our Victorian

forefathers, to talk with the people of a bygone era, to explore the quays, visit the village cooper and blacksmith, learn the vital part played by the assayer, take a train ride into the heart of the old George and Charlotte mine, or simply to soak up the serene beauty of the wood-lined banks of the winding river.

The riverside tramway takes visitors deep underground into the ancient copper mine so that they can see for themselves the conditions typical in a mine last worked in 1868. A giant water-wheel pumps away in the dark depths of the earth. *Son et lumiere* and *tableaux* depict the working conditions and technicalities of Victorian mining. The atmosphere of damp rock, the smell of gunpowder, tar and pine are all recreated to invoke lasting memories of this unusual experience. As their advertisements say, Morwellham really is unlike anywhere else in the modern world.

General Information

Owner: Morwellham Recreation Company Ltd
Title: Morwellham Quay – George and Charlotte Copper Mine
Location: Near Tavistock, West Devon. Map reference OS sheet 201 446697
Enquiries: The Manager, Morwellham Quay
Telephone: 0822 832766
Directions: From Tavistock take the A390, bear left 2 miles (3 kilometres) west of Tavistock.
Access: Open daily all year, 10 a.m.–6 p.m., except Christmas Day. Last admission 4.30 p.m. Winter season last admissions 2.30 p.m.
Nearest car park: Ample free car/coach parking on site
Distance: 660 yards (600 metres)
Time to explore: Two hours minimum. Guided tours half an hour.
Conditions: Graded, open air footpaths to Copper Mine Tramway station. Electric train takes visitors on a circular tour of the mine.
Facilities: Ship Inn licensed restaurant and tea rooms; Victorian sweetshop; museum shop; picnic area and lavatories. Explorer's guide leaflets and two historical trails: Red – ancient quay, mine and hydro-electric power station, horse and carriage; Blue – Victorian farmyard and Tavistock canal. Talk with people of the past in period costume; try on a costume; period photographs. Audio-visual presentation.
Parties: School parties and coach parties welcome.

Poldark Mine

Poldark Mine dates from about 1730 and was worked until 1810 after which it was closed. The only known reference to it is to be found on an 1856 plan in the County Records Office at Truro in which it is described as 'Wheal Roots, old men's workings' and was known to have five shafts and three levels. By the 1940s all trace of the mine had disappeared and it was only rediscovered by chance. When the site was purchased in 1966 there was little more to be seen than a couple of wooden huts and a large area of swamp land. It was not until the swamp had been drained with the idea of turning the place into a museum of industrial archeology, that the owners discovered there was a long forgotten mine literally underfoot. That was back in 1975 and since the following winter exploratory work underground has hardly ceased.

Initial access was obtained by way of East Shaft. Lowering the water-table had caused the back-filling to partially dry out, but before the levels of the old disused mine could be investigated, it was necessary to remove the earth and rubble accumulated over nigh on two centuries. Eventually the laborious task was completed and the excited team were able to descend into the dark, dank, wet, old workings. There was still a great deal of debris to be cleared before the mine was fit to be opened to the public, a job that was not only back-breaking but in an old mine for which there were no proper records, hair-raisingly dangerous, although the experience was not entirely without reward. As work proceeded in the narrow levels, old mining tools and equipment that had been lost or just left behind when the mine was abandoned were discovered. The most significant find was a child's wheelbarrow, the only one of its kind ever found; confirming that children under nine years of age regularly laboured down mines like Wheal Roots carting ore and spoil to surface before the Education Act of 1876 outlawed the practice.

Since the mine was first opened to the public on a limited scale, great strides have been made both on the surface and below ground. Visitors are now faced with a choice of two underground routes, both self-guided. There is a thoughtfully signposted short tour for the elderly and those with physical disabilities, which nevertheless gives a fair impression of the conditions with which the 'old men' had to contend centuries ago, and a longer, more adventurous route. The latter takes in all the tunnels and chambers which have so far been cleared including a viewing point at East Shaft which drops down to the third, as-yet-unexplored level. Here it is possible to gain a graphic impression of the fate which befell the miners trapped in the depths of the nearby Porkellis United Mine in 1858. This famous disaster was triggered by half a dozen miners breaking into an abandoned section and, unbeknown to the Mine Captain, removing quantities of rich ore from beneath a lake of discarded slimes to supplement their earnings. Eventually the inevitable happened; the roof of the section gave way flooding the entire mine with a glutinous suspension of mud and water to a depth of 250 feet (75 metres). The blast of air instantly blew out all candles, leaving some fifty miners to scramble to safety from the depths of the mine. It is a lasting tribute to the courage and fortitude of the Cornish miners that all but seven managed to escape from their man-made tomb and get back to 'grass' relatively unscathed.

General Information

Owner: Poldark Mining Company Ltd
Title: The Poldark Mine and Ha'Penny Park
Location: Wendron, near Helston, Cornwall
Enquiries: The Mine Manager
Telephone: 0326 573173
Directions: Wendron is 3 miles (4.8 kilometres) north of Helston on the B3297 to Redruth
Access: Open daily, Easter to October, 10 a.m.–6 p.m., August 10 a.m.–10 p.m.

Continued overleaf

Nearest car park: Ample free car/coach parking on site
Distance: 110 yards (100 metres)
Time to explore: One hour
Conditions: Poldark was once a working tin mine. In places it is wet and the roof is low. Protective headgear is provided free. The mine is unsuitable for the severely disabled. The surface exhibits are surrounded by paved footpaths.
Facilities: Pub, restaurants, cafeteria; souvenir shops, garden shop; museum; lavatories.

There is an impressive collection of tin mining artefacts and minerals on display in the museum. Surface exhibits include the giant 'Greensplat' beam engine, a saddle-tank locomotive and various stationary steam engines. Additional amusements are Non-Stop Pop Videos, Disco Boats, Stop the Clock, Inflatable Maze, Period Costume Photo Booth, Kiddy's Korner.
Parties: School and coach parties welcome.

Tilly Whim Caves

Durlston was established at Dorset's first country park in 1973. It is now part of the Purbeck Heritage Coast and is an Area of Outstanding Natural Beauty. But it was the late Victorians, with their increased prosperity and a penchant for taking sea-side holidays, who first made the caves and cliffs of Durlston into a rendezvous for tourists. The railway reached Swanage via Wareham and Corfe in 1885, bringing holiday-makers in their thousands to sample Dorset cream, sea-bathing and the serendipitous delights of a little gentle beach-combing. 'Taking the air' along the Tilly Whim Road or further west on the spectacular, and in rough weather decidedly dangerous, Dancing Ledge, became a popular pastime. And for the more scientifically minded there was fossil hunting; dinosaur footprints still occasionally come to light in local quarries.

It was in fact a Swanage stone merchant, George Burt, who first opened the area up to the public. In order to encourage buyers to speculate in a property development scheme, he had a network of cliff top paths, shrubberies and plantations laid out in the grounds of his Durlston Castle estate. There was even a romantic pine walk punctuated by a 'Great Globe', carved from a 39 ton (40 tonne) sphere of Portland Stone. When the project failed to attract buyers, he blasted a tunnel through the limestone so that visitors could scramble down to Tilly Whim and picnic on the rocks. Evidently something of a pioneer conservationist, Burt, a stickler for detail, even had inscriptions carved into the rock face conveying such messages as: 'look around and read great nature's open book' and 'please protect the

wildfowl and other birds', together with extracts from the scriptures and poems to impress upon the wide-eyed members of the public the awesome forces of nature, a sensible precaution for Tilly Whim can change character dramatically. When the sun hides behind the pines and a south-westerly gale sends towering seas crashing against the rocks, raining salt spray over the craggy cliff tops and distorting the stubborn, stunted trees and bushes into bizarre forms, wise people stay indoors.

There are in all four separate trails to follow at Durlston Country Park. To view Tilly Whim in its magnificent cliffside setting, however, it is necessary to take the Cliff Top Trail. This leads westwards from the car park and Information Centre to the cliff path and from there proceeds eastwards towards the Anvil Point Lighthouse. At several points along the foot of the cliffs there are various small sea caves to be seen, but these have been formed by the natural action of wind and tide. The Tilly Whim Caves are entirely man-made, having once been an extensive underground quarry.

The caves themselves are currently not open to the public, but from close by the lighthouse, visible for 24 miles (38 kilometres) out to sea on a clear night, it is possible to look down to the stepped terraces of the old workings. The highly sought after Portland Stone was originally worked from natural ledges and, having been cut out of the cliffs, was lowered into waiting boats by a crane or 'whim' and transported to the stone yards at Swanage for further working. As more and more stone was removed, so it became necessary for the quarrymen to excavate deeper into the rock face, forming an interconnecting labyrinth of caves and tunnels beneath the cliffs. It was during the eighteenth century that rumours of smuggling became rife. Many of the quarrymen were associated with smuggling and where better to hide contraband than in the maze of workings they knew like the back of their hands? The quarries fell into disuse during the Napoleonic wars, but local folklore maintains that smuggling went on well into the nineteenth century.

Little has changed since Victorian times and the abundant wildlife living in and around the limestone cliffs continues to prove a source of considerable pleasure and interest for ornithologists. Here can be seen fulmars, guillemots, kittiwakes, razorbills, shags and gulls. At breeding times the seabirds crowd together in raucous colonies, flying constant sorties to their feeding grounds. On the cliffs and rocky paths thrift and sea campion cling precariously to clefts in the rocks, and, thankfully, just as in Burt's time, on a good day the bracing quality of the air has a magic about it that is almost tangible.

General Information

Owner: Dorset County Council
Title: Tilly Whim Caves
Location: The Cliff Top Trail, Durlston Country Park, Swanage, Dorset. Map reference OS sheet 195 031770
Enquiries: The Warden, Durlston Country Park
Telephone: 0929 424443
Directions: Proceed through Swanage to the end of Institute Road. Turn right into Seymer Road, right again into Peverel Road and finally Durlston Road.
Access: The Tilly Whim Caves are currently not open to the public. The Cliff Top Trail is open daily all year. Durlston Country Park Centre is open from Easter to October.
Nearest car park: Car parking on site. There is a nominal charge for parking from Easter to October. At other times parking is free. Coach tour organizers should contact the Park Information Centre during peak holiday periods.
Distance: The Cliff Top Trail is one mile (1.5 kilometres) in length. Tilly Whim is approximately half-way round.
Time to explore: One hour
Conditions: The footpaths are mainly surfaced. There is one very steep section. The cliffs can be dangerous; visitors are advised to stay on the path and keep well away from the cliff edge.
Facilities: Durlston Country Park Information Centre has an informative display showing the history of the area with details of the local flora and fauna. A series of information leaflets are available at a nominal charge. Lavatories. There is a licensed restaurant and café at Durlston Castle. Guided tours are available during the summer season. The park includes an area of Special Scientific Interest. For further details contact the Head Warden.
Parties: School and coach parties welcome by prior arrangement.

Wheal Coates

Rivalled only by Trewavas on the south coast near Helston, the view looking west past the ruins of Wheal Coates along the Cornwall North Coast Path towards Godrevy Point must surely rank as one of the most photogenic panoramas in the whole of Cornwall. Situated half-way down the cliff face, the main engine house stands beside the 670 feet (205 metres) deep Towanroath Engine Shaft into which the sea broke many years ago. For reasons of safety this has recently been capped with a grille. Nevertheless, in rough weather, spray can be seen emanating from the top, accompanied by menacing sounds of subterranean percussion as the Atlantic breakers funnel into the adit. This never particularly prosperous mine was worked for both tin and copper spasmodically for most of the last century. During the 1870s the building which was restored by the Nat-

ional Trust housed a 36 inch (91 centimetre) beam pumping engine, later replaced by one of horizontal pattern. Although there was an attempt to reopen the mine in 1911, it was last effectively worked in 1889.

It is possible to view the adit itself at low tide. The safest way to do this is to proceed to Chapel Porth and walk back along the fine sandy beach. The original drainage tunnel would have been relatively small, but more than a century of battering by the sea has opened it up so that it looks for all the world like an enormous sea cave. Stretching darkly back into the cliff, it invites investigation, but once one invades the hushed gloom of its inner reaches, an ominous chill pervades the air. This, coupled with the sepulchral trickle of discoloured mine water which still issues from the hidden depths of the old workings, encourages

Continued overleaf

a distinct sense of unease. Beware too that this is not a place to be trapped by the incoming tide.

General Information

Owner: National Trust
Title: Wheal Coates
Location: St Agnes Beacon, St Agnes, North Cornwall. Map reference OS sheet 203 700502
Enquiries: National Trust Regional Office, Lanhydrock, Bodmin, Cornwall

Telephone: 0208 4281
Directions: Take the footpath off the road between St Agnes Head and Chapel Porth.
Access: Any reasonable time
Nearest car park: Free car parking on site
Distance: 440 yards (400 metres)
Time to explore: Half an hour
Conditions: Rough, open cliff-top site. Stout footwear is recommended. Always beware of unfenced cliffs, mine shafts and unstable masonry.
Facilities: None.

THE CHANNEL ISLANDS

GUERNSEY

Underground
Hospital

La Valette
Underground
Military Museum

JERSEY

Underground
Strawberry Farm ● Hospital

La Hougue
Bie

La Corbiere

Noirmont
Point

Emerging from the shallow continental shelf off the coast of Brittany, the Channel Islands have an exotic character all their own which is neither French nor wholly British. Blessed with a balmy climate that is sufficiently different to that on the mainland for flowers and agricultural produce to be grown out of season, it is perhaps not surprising that Hitler saw their occupation not only in terms of a thorn in Churchill's side, but as a future off-shore holiday resort for the German people once the war was over.

When Hitler gave his notable 20th October 1941 directive that: 'The permanent fortifying of the Channel Islands to convert them into an impregnable fortress must be pressed forward at maximum speed', it was perfectly clear to everyone concerned that the term permanent meant precisely that. In no time at all, it must have seemed to the embattled islanders, forts, bunkers, command headquarters, machine-gun posts, tank traps and shore-line obstacles

were sprouting from the sand and soil like weeds after a deluge. To augment local labour the Organization Todt was imported and soon there were camps full of conscripted foreign workers and, even more depressing, slaves. Fortified out of all proportion to their size, the islands became the western corner-stone of Hitler's Atlantic Wall.

The Germans, noted for their thoroughness, did not mess about. If the Third Reich was going to last a thousand years, the fortifications needed to be constructed accordingly. Luckily for the inhabitants of the Channel Islands, Hitler's ambitions were thwarted after just a few years; whether the reinforced mass concrete legacy of his Atlantic Wall will survive the next millenia is open to conjecture. Judging by the age of the much less solidly constructed La Hougue Bie, a prehistoric tomb believed to date from 3,000 BC, by the look of things they just could become one of the wonders of the world in the year AD 3,000.

Guernsey Underground Hospital

Guernsey's German Military Underground Hospital and Ammunition Store is the most extensive example of the many underground installations left behind by the German occupation of the Channel Islands. First opened to the public in 1954, this damp, forbidding, 1.25 miles (2 kilometres) warren of largely empty

echoing corridors and wards covers an area of some 75,000 square feet (7,000 square metres). All but invisible from the surface, the concrete and brick maze is built beneath a low hill in the heart of the picturesque Guernsey countryside. Constructed by the Organization Todt, hundreds of volunteers and slave workers from

Continued overleaf

all over Europe laboured around the clock for three and a half years to excavate, concrete and equip the place. Yet after all their efforts it was only ever in use for nine months.

Unlike its sister establishment on Jersey, the Guernsey installation was planned to be part hospital, part munitions store. Designed to accommodate 500, in emergency the hospital section could have housed at least 1,500 in addition to the necessary doctors, nurses and ancillaries needed to staff the place. Although for the most part only used for storage, part of it was actually put to use as a hospital after the D-Day landings when a few hundred German wounded, brought over from France, were treated on the premises. Their stay was not an altogether beneficial experience. Many claimed that their kit became mildewed over-night due to the high humidity and excessive condensation which even the ingenious German central heating and ventilation system could not overcome. It is said that after three or four weeks those that survived emerged as white as their bed-sheets! Of course their condition may well have been aggravated by the knowledge that they were sharing their concrete molehill with thousands of tons of high explosive, covered with tarpaulins to keep it dry. Then, as now, condensation was a serious problem.

The layout consists of two parallel main corridors linked by wards, an operating theatre, X-ray room, laboratory, dispensary, store rooms, staff sleeping quarters, a cinema and a mortuary. Although most of the original equipment was removed by the original owners and the Allies, much of the central heating plant is still *in situ*; originally the installation had its own generating plant to drive the gas-proof air-conditioning system. There are also hospital beds and the remains of the kitchen. To visit the premises now is a most curious experience. The dank, dark, echoing corridors, shining with condensation, seem to go on for ever and the feeling of hopeless gloom that pervades the place is not made any better by the knowledge that during construction rock falls and at least one explosion resulted in the deaths of numerous members of the slave labour force who were forced to work or starve. Those too weak to work were transferred to the notorious Lager Sylt on Alderney, the only German concentration camp to have been built on British soil.

General Information

Owner: Mr and Mrs J Browning
Title: The German Military Underground Hospital and Ammunition Store
Location: La Vassalerie Road, St Andrew's, Guernsey, C.I. Map reference OS series M824 Guernsey 308769
Enquiries: Mrs J Browning
Telephone: 0481 39100
Directions: From St Peter Port take the Mont Durrant/St Andrew's Road. Take the first turning left after passing St Andrew's Parish Church, 270 yards (250 metres) into La Vassalerie Road and the hospital is approximately 220 yards (200 metres) on the right.
Access: Open to the public from March to October, seven days a week, and November, December and February, Thursdays and Sundays. In January the hospital is closed. Opening hours 9.30 a.m.–5.30 p.m. Last admission 4.15 p.m.
Nearest car park: Small free car park opposite the main entrance
Distance: Entrance 55 yards (50 metres) from car park
Time to explore: One hour
Conditions: Level hard surfaces throughout suitable for wheelchairs. At certain times of year the tunnels are sometimes rather wet underfoot.
Facilities: Museum of occupation relics and newspapers; gift shop.
Parties: Coach and school parties are welcome.

Jersey Underground Hospital

Besides being the most widely known of all the relics of the Occupation, the Jersey Underground Hospital is arguably the most intriguing and certainly the most controversial. This particular tunnel project, officially designated *Hohlgangsanlage Nummer 8* (HO 8), was not originally planned as a hospital at all, but as an *Artillerie Unterknuft* – a vast subterranean artillery barracks and gun maintenance workshop – the idea being that it should be annexed to the main infantry base at St Peter's. But the project was dogged by problems from the start.

Work began at Cap Verd in 1941, but did not get into full swing until the summer of the following year. The main obstacle to progress was the substrata which consisted of Briovarian shale. Known as 'mud stone' it had the reputation of being a particularly treacherous material to blast. Handled by the motley collection of largely unskilled labour the Organization Todt assembled, it proved to be down right dangerous. The more apocryphal stories, including the coach-driver's favourite that SS guards with whips and alsatians ordered those too weak to lift a shovel to be thrown into the concrete shuttering wholesale, are both historically inaccurate and unnecessarily sensational. No members of the SS ever served on Jersey. Nevertheless the fact remains that the working conditions were appalling and the predominantly foreign work force, many of whom were literally slaves, were treated with stone-faced barbarism.

Mining is one of the most dangerous jobs in the world at the best of times and with their sorry condition aggravated by meagre rations, appalling accommodation and lack of adequate, let alone protective, clothing, accidents were commonplace. Even so, the only substantiated account of men being permanently buried where they worked was as a result of a disastrous rock fall which occurred in a side tunnel off the present entrance at Meadowbank. In spite of every effort being made to free the trapped men, it proved an impossible task. Work on that section was therefore discontinued and the spur walled up.

But how did HO 8 come to be a hospital? Well before the project was due to be completed, cracks were already beginning to show in Hitler's great master plan for world domination. Precisely when the paranoic powers that be decided the tunnels would make a handy hospital is not recorded, but as rumours of a D-Day of some sort were rapidly becoming a reality, someone must have seen a need for a secure emergency casualty unit on Jersey as well as Guernsey. HO 8 was deep, gas-proof, and at a push, capable of housing several thousand men. It must have seemed ideal.

In a short space of time the completed sections of the one mile (1.6 kilometres) of tunnels were cleared and fitted out as a hospital. But conditions inside were far from ideal and in the event HO 8 only served briefly as a casualty clearing station during the period following the Allied advance into France. The main problem was condensation. Therefore, when the Allied invasion of Normandy never so much as rattled an enamel theatre bowl on Jersey, the German military doctors decreed that the crisis had passed and promptly evacuated their anaemic-looking patients to the General Hospital. Fear of being bombed or shelled was preferable to being cooped up in a labyrinth of sweating, concrete-lined tunnels, air-conditioned or not.

Since the Liberation, the fortunes, and the character, of the Underground Hospital have changed considerably. The new owners have, as far as possible, recreated the layout, if not precisely the grim air of reality, that would have been prevalent in 1944. Nevertheless with a little imagination the visitor can step back in time and visualize the Kommandant's Office, the Doctor's Quarters, the Officers' Mess and the Operating Theatre much as they were during that momentous summer nearly half a century ago.

General Information

Owners: Sanctuary Inns Ltd
Title: The Jersey German Underground Hospital
Location: Meadowbank, St Peter's Valley, Jersey, C.I.
Enquiries: The Curator, German Underground Hospital
Telephone: 0534 63442
Directions: From Bel Royal drive up St Peter's Valley (A11) for about one mile (1.6 kilometres). Turn right at Tesson Mill (B89) for Meadow Bank and follow the signposts.
Access: Open to the public from March to October seven days a week, and November, December and February, Thursdays and Sundays. In January the hospital is closed. Opening hours 9.30 a.m.–5.30 p.m. Last admission 4.15 p.m.
Nearest car park: Ample car/coach park opposite main entrance.
Distance: 55 yards (50 metres)
Time to explore: One or two hours
Conditions: Dry and level hard surfaces throughout suitable for wheelchairs.
Facilities: Lavatories, including facilities for the disabled. Gift shop. Refreshments are available nearby.
Parties: School and coach parties welcome.

La Corbiere, Jersey

In 1941, after failing to convince the British of the inherent advantages of joining the Third Reich the previous summer, Hitler turned his martial, megalomanic mind towards Russia. But, having lost the Battle of Britain, more by misjudgement than luck, despite his preoccupations in the east, innate paranoia cautioned against leaving himself vulnerable to the west. There then followed a whole series of fortification directives culminating in the stipulation that the Channel Islands were to be incorporated into the Atlantic Wall defence complex. In the event money became no object and over a period of two years or so the islands became veritable gun-platforms, more intensely fortified than any other comparable section of the 'Wall'.

That the instigator of the project was the Fuhrer is beyond doubt. But it seems likely that those who were saddled with the executive responsibility for making his scheme concrete, could not have failed to be aware that the more work they could find to do in the balmy Bay of St Malo, the less likelihood there was of being posted to the Russian front. As a direct result, the unfortunate islanders found themselves reluctant hosts for not only large numbers of German army, navy and air-force personnel, but for the ubiquitous Organization Todt together with their gangs of foreign, volunteer and forced labour as well. While, initially, much of the preliminary emplacement work had been carried out by members of the German armed services aided by local labour, when it was decided to make the islands into an impregnable bastion, the Organization Todt became responsible for most of the actual building work involved in realizing Hitler's obsessive master plan.

The casemate of the La Corbiere bunker was built to house one of eighty-four *Canon de 105 mle 1913 Schneider* the Germans deployed to fortify the Channel Islands during their four-year term of occupation. Manufactured at the Le Creuset works, now more famous for cooking utensils than armaments, many of these guns were captured when the French Army capitulated in 1941. Redesignated 10.5 cm K331(f) and converted for fortress use by the addition of a central pivot and an armoured shield, eighteen of them were emplaced around the Jersey coastline in a series of strategically sited casemates.

The massive reinforced concrete blockhouse itself was constructed in 1943 and well displays the characteristics of contemporary Organization Todt architecture. These monolithic masterpieces were cast to a standard design which could be varied to suit the topography and terrain. Hitler dictated that '... the strength of the fortifications ... will be based on the principles and practical knowledge gained from building the Western Wall' – on which, admittedly, the Allies subsequently hung their washing, but not through any fault of the designers! As sound as the day it was built over forty-five years ago, with 6.5 feet (2 metre) thick ceilings and walls, radiused to deflect direct hits, this example of Dr Fritz Todt's practical interpretation of the Fuhrer's demand for 'fortress standards' speaks as eloquently for the art of function before form as any blockhouse in history.

Perhaps by virtue of its difficult access, it retains not only its original armoured doors, the seals of which are still gas-proof, but much other original equipment such as ventilation and electrical fittings, wall-cladding and telephones, not to mention the original 'canon' of which there are only five surviving examples. Much work was nevertheless required to bring the place up to the current standard of originality, but thanks to the enthusiasm of the members of the Channel Island Occupation Society and with the aid of a grant from the Jersey Heritage Trust, it has been possible to reintroduce electric light, replace the wall-cladding and reline the gun-room with wood.

General Information

Owner: States of Jersey Department of Public Building and Works
Title: The La Corbiere 105 millimetre Casemate Bunker
Location: La Corbiere, St Brelade, Jersey, C.I. Map reference OS sheet Jersey 555481
Enquiries: Honorary Secretary, Channel Islands Occupational Society (CIOS), 'Rangistacy', Grouville, Jersey, C.I.
Telephone: 0534 54383
Directions: From St Brelade take the A13 and proceed to La Moye. Turn left onto the B83 and follow direction signs to La Corbiere.
Access: Open to the public from April to October on Saturdays, 11 a.m.–4 p.m.
Nearest car park: Free car park on adjoining open space at La Corbiere Head.
Distance: Entrance 55 yards (50 metres) west of the parking area

Time to explore: Allow one hour
Conditions: Dry and level hard surfaces throughout. To gain access to the bunker it is necessary to descend a short flight of stairs. The emplacement is unsuitable for the severely disabled.
Facilities: Bookstall well stocked with Occupation and CIOS publications.
Guided tours can be arranged if required. Contact the Honorary Secretary for further information.
The interior of the casemate has been restored as nearly as possible to the original condition. It still contains the original 105 millimetre K331(F) gun. All maintenance and restoration work is carried out by CIOS volunteers in their own time, using money raised by members' subscriptions, sales of publications and donations by the public.
Parties: Coach and school parties are welcome during normal opening hours.

La Hougue Bie, Jersey

Set in beautiful grounds dominated by a grassy mound 40 feet (14 metres) high, La Hougue Bie is one of the finest Neolithic ritual burial sites in western Europe. In the middle of the mound there is a great chamber some 30 feet (9 metres) long, 10 feet (3 metres) wide and averaging approximately 6.5 feet (2 metres) high, with three side cells approached by a tapering passage 33 feet (10 metres) in length. The side walls are constructed from massive upright stones known as orthostats. These were manoeuvered into position and set into the ground by means of earth ramps, wooden rollers and, presumably a degree of brute strength. These stones were in turn capped by progressively larger cover stones of which the largest is estimated to weigh over 24.6 tons (25 tonnes).

A curious characteristic of the chamber, with its north, south and west cells set out in the form of a cross, is that, in both orientation and in layout, it bears remarkable similarities to a church with a nave, side chapels and a chancel. This has given rise to the theory that at the time it was built, *circa* 3500 BC, it may well have been used for some complex religious purpose besides being a tomb. When the chamber was excavated in 1924 it became obvious that it had been previously pillaged, and pillaged very thoroughly, in the remote past. Sadly, so little of archeological import had been left behind that

the few finds, which included the scattered remains of perhaps as many as eight individuals, far from providing useful evidence as to the precise use to which the mound and its cruciform subterranean chamber had been put, if anything deepened the mystery. It has been suggested that there might well be further hidden chambers concealed beneath the mound; certainly dowsing there has been successful so this possibility is less than remote.

The Neolithic mound was probably built in a series of stepped mounds retained by drystone walling brought from Queen's Valley, 1 mile (1.5 kilometres) away, but over the years it has been rounded by erosion. The medieval building sitting on top of the mound in reality consists of two chapels: the Notre Dame de la Clarte which dates from the twelfth century and the Jerusalem chapel some four centuries later. Both buildings were extensively repaired and partly rebuilt in 1924. The building may be approached by way of a spiral ramp. In summer the view from the top is obscured by foliage, but in winter, on a clear day, the vantage point affords a splendid view of the greater part of the island plateau. To the west of the mound there is a Museum of the German Occupation in an original German underground shelter. An excellent display of old agricultural machinery and artefacts is to be

Continued overleaf

found on the other side of the small car park. The site also houses the island's main archeological and geological exhibits and an old guard's van of the now defunct Jersey Eastern Railways.

The Jersey Museums Trust is run jointly by the Société Jersaise and the Jersey Heritage Trust. In addition to its primary responsibilities, it also provides a museum information service, arranges numerous special events and exhibitions and is involved in the general conservation and interpretation of the island's heritage.

General Information

Owner: Société Jersaise
Title: La Hougue Bie Museum
Location: La Hougue Bie, Grouville, Jersey, C.I. Map reference OS sheet Jersey 683503
Enquiries: The Director, La Hougue Bie Museum
Telephone 0534 53823

Bookings for school/group visits should be made through the Education Officer, Jersey Museum Service, 9 Pier Road, St Helier. Telephone 63333.
Directions: From St Helier take the Mount Millais Road to Five Oaks. Continue along Princes Tower Road to the site entrance. Bus route number 3A from St Helier.
Access: Open March to October, Tuesday to Sunday 10 a.m.–5 p.m.
Nearest car park: Limited free car parking on site. Roadside parking is permitted when the car park is full.
Distance: 22 yards (20 metres)
Time to explore: Tomb half an hour, museum one and a half hours.
Conditions: Dry, level gravel footpaths throughout. Headroom at the tomb entrance is barely 3 feet (1 metre) increasing to standing headroom in the main chamber.
Facilities: Refreshments, snacks, sweets, tea and coffee machine.
Pleasant gardens. Medieval chapels. Museum of agricultural history, archeology and geology. German underground shelter and Occupation Museum. Jersey Eastern Railway guard's van. Old granite weights.
Parties: School parties and coach parties welcome by arrangement. The Education Officer will advise local and visiting schools, colleges and groups on visits and activities. Guided tours and information sheets are available on request from Jersey Museum Service.

La Valette Underground Military Museum, Guernsey

La Valette is one of the more recent additions to the list of Channel Island attractions dealing with war memorabilia. The tunnel complex which houses this brand new museum was originally built by the Germans during the Occupation. The tunnels were designed and built in order to house four enormous horizontal tanks to hold diesel oil for the purpose of refuelling U-Boats. The tanks themselves were built in Bremen in Germany to hold approximately 30,000 gallons (136,000 litres) of fuel oil each. Only one tank remains in the tunnel; the other three are at various locations about the island and still in everyday use.

Underground installations are, by and large, notoriously wet, particularly if they are not well ventilated. Virtually all the tunnels the Germans built on the islands during World War Two suffered from condensation and leaching ground-water in some degree. La Valette was no exception, parts of it literally running with water, so much so that a less

promising environment conducive to the long term preservation and display of what are, essentially, bio-degradable exhibits, would have been difficult to find. Strenuous efforts were made to overcome this problem, using modern materials to water-proof the mass concrete lining which had become porous over the years. Although it has taken approximately three years to convert the fuel storage tunnels into a museum, the results have more than justified all the trouble, and with the installation of an air-conditioning system to control temperature and humidity the many valuable exhibits on display now enjoy a near perfect environment.

In addition to making the place more comfortable and water-tight than its original builders could ever have imagined possible, every effort has been made to keep the interior looking authentic, even down to using the original light fittings to create the characteristic utilitarian atmosphere of the original installation.

The displays include a comprehensive collection of war-time memorabilia including a realistic camouflage gun emplacement, a number of military vehicles and an assortment of regimental uniforms. The detailed effort that has gone into this compact museum speaks for itself; would that every museum curator could have such well thought out and well controlled conditions in which to display exhibits.

General Information

Owner: PGP Ltd
Title: La Valette Underground Museum

Location: Houlgang 4, La Valette, St Peter Port, Guernsey, C.I.
Enquiries: G. Przenislawski, Managing Director
Telephone: 0481 22300
Directions: From St Peter Port Bus Terminal walk towards the bathing pool at La Valette. Four or five minutes walk.
Access: Open daily all year 10 a.m.–5.30 p.m.
Nearest car park: No parking on site. Limited roadside parking permitted at site.
Distance: 33 feet (10 metres)
Time to explore: One hour minimum
Conditions: Dry concrete paths throughout. The tunnel is air-conditioned. There are several short flights of stairs.
Facilities: A comprehensive display centred around Guernsey's military history. The tunnel is surrounded by a pleasant natural area with magnificent views out to sea and of the neighbouring islands.
Parties: School parties and coach parties welcome. Guided tours available by arrangement.

Noirmont Point, Jersey

The Batterie Lothringen was one of a total of five coastal installations built for the Marine Artillerie Abteilung during the German Occupation. The southern-most link in the Channel Island's Atlantic Wall defences, whilst not possessing the formidable 20 mile (32 kilometre) clout of the 12 inch (305 millimetre) Batterie Mirus on Guernsey, its four strategically placed 5.9 inch (150 millimetre) guns nevertheless effectively kept the surrounding seas free from Allied shipping from March 1941 until the end of the War. Initially the battery operated from temporary positions until permanent gun platforms, ammunition bunkers and personnel shelters were constructed. But once the complex was completed, with its naval direction-finding equipment, attendant search-lights and flack emplacements, plus a total of sixteen fixed flame-throwers set amongst the barbed-wire and the mine-fields, this particular promontory became a very hostile place indeed.

Built on a ledge blasted out of the cliffs, the artillery Command Bunker took the Organization Todt just over a year to complete. One of four similar units designed to house precision range-finding equipment, the others being fort Mirus on Guernsey and batteries Annes and Elsass on Alderney, the Noirmont Bunker was commissioned in April 1944. Unfortunately, after the Islands were liberated in May 1945, the installation was systematically stripped of most of its equipment by souvenir hunters, the British Army and a succession of builders and scrap dealers. Following an accident to an intrepid individual who attempted to explore its subterranean depths in the dark, in 1948 the building, by then little more than an echoing empty shell, was sealed up. It remained thus until 1977 when the Channel Islands Occupation Society obtained permission to reopen the bunker with a view to restoring the interior to as near original condition as possible and opening it to the general public.

A close inspection of Noirmont Point makes Hitler's dream seem chillingly real, even now, particularly when one ventures underground. The Lothringen Bunker is surprisingly extensive and has something of the atmosphere of an ancient Egyptian tomb about it. Perhaps this has something to do with the means of access which is by way of a long, dark, silent staircase, unique to this particular installation, extending downwards for some 39 feet (12 metres). After passing the sinister lower entrance defence gun ports and stepping over the threshold of the gas-tight doors, visitors enter the bunker proper. Sadly, the past depredations of the scrap-metal merchants have resulted in the massive armoured range-finder housing and turret being lost forever. However, the dual armoured steel periscope cupolas still remain

Continued overleaf

and, standing in the operations room, it is possible to imagine what it would feel like to serve in such a placement when under attack. Not that those who served at Noirmont saw very much action. Made only too well aware of the potential destructive power of the Channel Island emplacements by reconnaissance reports, generally speaking Allied shipping kept a wide berth for most of the war. Consequently, during their brief heyday, the guns of Lothringen spoke in anger only once – the night of 13th June 1944 when the accurate and sustained firepower of the battery drove off HMS *Ashanti* and a free Polish destroyer.

Just as in a contemporary battleship, the fire-control officer and his assistants collated the data from their sophisticated instruments and relayed it to the four guns on their platforms outside by telephone. The communications network was both elaborate and efficient, it being possible for the occupants of the bunker to enjoy direct communication with the other artillery batteries, observation towers, the Island Artillery Commander at St Peter and the Naval Commander, Channel Islands, at his HQ at St Jacques in Guernsey.

A further flight of stairs leads to the lower level which once contained crews' quarters and plant rooms. These were relatively well fitted out as those manning the bunker were subject to a monthly time-table of three weeks on and one week off. When off-duty they were quartered at houses nearby; the artillerymen who manned the guns being billeted in what is now Jersey Holiday Village at Portlet. The CIOS have made contact with several erstwhile members of the various war-time crews, some of whom still return to Jersey on holiday to revisit their old bunker and give authentic advice on the building's restoration.

General Information

Owners: States of Jersey Department of Public Building and Works
Title: The Noirmont Command Bunker
Location: Noirmont Point, St. Brelade, Jersey, C.I. Map reference OS sheet Jersey 607466
Enquiries: Honorary Secretary Channel Islands Occupation Society (CIOS), 'Rangistacy', Grouville, Jersey, C.I.
Telephone: 0534 54383
Directions: From St. Aubin take the A13 and proceed for about one mile (1.6 kilometres). Turn left onto the B57 and follow direction signs to Noirmont Point. The Command Bunker is 55 yards (50 metres) due north of the Direction Finding Tower on the headland.
Access: Open to the public Thursday evenings, 7 p.m.–9.30 p.m. during June, July and August
Nearest car park: Free car park on adjoining open space
Distance: Entrance 55 yards (50 metres) from parking area
Time to explore: Allow one hour
Conditions: Dry and level hard surfaces throughout. To gain access to the bunker it is necessary to descend a flight of stairs. The bunker is unsuitable for the severely disabled.
Facilities: Bookstall well stocked with Occupation and CIOS publications. Guided tours can be arranged if required. Contact the Honorary Secretary for further information. The interior of the bunker is in the process of being restored as nearly as possible to the original condition. The headland contains numerous remains of Batterie Lothringen and provides spectacular views of the bays of Portelet, St Brelade and St Aubin and the approaches to St Helier.
Parties: Coach and school parties are welcome during normal opening hours.

Strawberry Farm, Jersey

Situated at the heart of the Strawberry Farm Holiday Park complex is one of the many almost indestructible relics of the Nazi occupation. This building, one of five virtually identical Kernwerk command and communications bunkers on the island, formed an integral part of the German 'Atlantic Wall' defences which stretched from the North Cape of Norway to the Spanish border, and from 1942 until 1945 was the Inselkommandant's (Jersey) Battle Headquarters. Described by the Nazi propaganda machine as: '. . . this battleship of concrete and steel anchored in front of the main Atlantic Wall', the attendant artillery installations on Jersey, Guernsey and Alderney effectively sealed off the Gulf of St Malo attack by sea.

Obviously inter-island communication was at a premium. Each bunker in the complex was linked by an elaborate telephone switchboard coordinating the artillery defence installation for the whole of Jersey, linked to every single battery, stronghold and military unit in the island. There was also a radio communications

A rare opportunity to see a working underground water-wheel deep in the old George and Charlotte Mine at Morwellham (page 45)

Dating from the 1830s this horizontal tandem steam engine once powered a brickworks but now runs on compressed air in the engine house at Poldark (page 47)

Above
The gunners of the La Corbiere casemate, Jersey, doubtless slept more soundly knowing that their fully air-conditioned accommodation was also gas proof . . . (page 54)

Below
The irregular cruciform chamber at the centre of the 5000-year-old La Hougue Bie, Jersey's spectacular neolithic ritual burial mound (page 55)

network to similar artillery Command Headquarters on the neighbouring islands and to the headquarters of the Naval Commander in Chief (Channel Islands) based on Guernsey.

The Command Bunker was reputed to have a direct phone line to Hitler, but this rumour proved to be something of an exaggeration. It was also said to be linked by tunnel to the Underground Hospital, but there is no evidence for this either. Such rumours no doubt ran rife on the island during the Occupation – hardly surprising when a policy of ultra-secrecy on pain of death was obligatory for enforcers and enforced alike. In reality the only direct line from the bunker was to Divisional HQ on Guernsey. To speak to the Fuhrer in person it would have been necessary to be linked via a second undersea cable to 84th Army Corps HQ at St Lo on the French mainland. From there the call could have been relayed to Berlin and indeed, if of sufficient gravity, to Adolf himself, but it would have to have been important!

Intriguingly enough the *Kreigsmarine* (navy) had signals priority and were able to get through directly to Wilhelmshaven. Nevertheless the artillery communications system was very sophisticated for its time and included an 'enigma' machine, the very hush hush, electromechanical cipher device that proved impossible to decode by conventional methods. After much experimentation and the expenditure of considerable midnight oil, the British 'back room boys' at Bletchley Park eventually managed to crack the system, inadvertently inventing what was arguably the world's first practical computer in the process. There is an original enigma machine at the St Peter's Bunker Occupation Museum.

Bunkers of the Strawberry Farm pattern were built by the Organization Todt, in accordance with Type 609 (Army Divisional Command Bunkers), modified as necessary to suit the local topography. Similar constructions can be found along the length of the Atlantic Wall and throughout Europe. The external walls and roofs of these monolithic reinforced concrete structures were a minimum of 6.5 feet (2 metres) thick and designed not only to withstand a direct hit from a 1,000 pound (450 kilogramme) bomb, but to 'bounce' in the event of a near miss. To reduce the possibility of shock-waves causing chunks of concrete 'shrapnel' to flake off the ceiling during bombardment injuring the personnel inside, steel 'mesh' was incorporated in the soffit of the mass concrete. As a further refinement internal rooms all featured heavy steel doors with seals of artificial rubber which in most cases are every bit as gas-proof today as they were when first installed over forty-five years ago!

Because of their bulky silhouette, characterized by the 6.5 feet (2 metre) radius quadrant at the 'eaves' intended to deflect glancing hits by shells and bombs, the purpose of these buildings was all too obvious. In order to effect a small deception the ingenious Germans therefore made a practice of disguising them as cottages by adding chimneys, pitched tiled roofs, false timber gables and painting the walls with pretend windows to which they added mock shutters. They wouldn't have fooled an estate agent let alone the eagle-eyes of Allied Intelligence. But then the Allies were quite happy for Hitler to reinforce this section of his pet defence system since it meant that he could not use the materials elsewhere where they might prove more of a nuisance.

The building was intended to be staffed and run by a crew of between five and seven on a planned duty rota which could mean being underground for three weeks at a time. To keep vital maps and equipment free from damp and condensation it was equipped with a coal-fired central-heating system, together with a self-contained ventilation and air purification system designed to protect the occupants from a gas attack. The wiring and wooden wainscot lining on much of the inside walls is all original and for connoisseurs of German bunker architecture there is a unique wooden hand-rail on the staircase – usually this item was made of steel. The installation is also interesting in that it had its own well and water storage system with a pumping bunker on the opposite side of the road. There was also a dry moat crossed by

Continued overleaf

steel draw-bridges and covered by a re-entrant heavy machine-gun emplacement, not to mention fully equipped *waschraum und abort*, complete with flushing toilets, and yes, since you ask, the drains do still work!

After so much thought, trouble, ingenuity and effort had been put into the design and construction of Strawberry Farm and its Channel Island siblings to make them well-nigh impregnable, it almost seems an anti-climax to learn that these impressive defences were only ever used during exercises and for a few brief weeks after D-Day. Like the defenders of the French Maginot line, the Island Commanders were forced to stand listening helplessly to the distant rumble of guns, unable to up-anchor and join in the fray when the Mulberry Harbours of the Normandy Beach-head passed them by. Perhaps it was as well.

General Information

Owner: The Jersey Strawberry Holiday Park (1984) Ltd
Title: German WWII Underground HQ
Location: Jersey Strawberry Farm, Rue de Petit Aleval, St Peter's Valley, Jersey
Enquiries: Mrs. Spears
Telephone: 0534 81273
Directions: From Bel Royal drive up St Peter's Valley (A11) for about 3 miles (4.8 kilometres). Turn right into Mont De L'Ecole (C112). At the top of the hill turn right and the entrance is straight ahead.
Access: Open to the public from March to October 10 a.m.–5.30 p.m.
Nearest car park: Own large free car park
Distance: Entrance 110 yards (100 metres) from car park
Time to explore: Half an hour bunker, two hours for complete complex
Conditions: Dry and level hard surfaces throughout. To gain access to the lower bunker level it is necessary to descend a flight of stairs.
Facilities: The German bunker is surrounded by well laid out grounds with paved pathways wide enough for wheelchairs. Disabled person's lavatories are available. Self-service cafeteria specializing in strawberry cream teas; jacket potato bar; fully licensed covered barbecue. In addition to the German War Museum there are various other attractions including: Craft Centre, French Boules, Children's Playground, Pets' Corner, Miniature Village, Eighteen-hole Putting Green.
Parties: Coach and school parties are welcome

THE SOUTH MIDLANDS

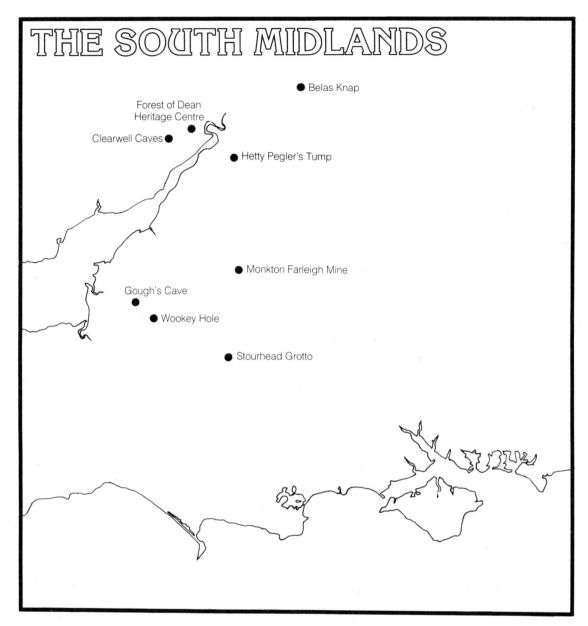

- Belas Knap
- Forest of Dean Heritage Centre
- Clearwell Caves
- Hetty Pegler's Tump
- Monkton Farleigh Mine
- Gough's Cave
- Wookey Hole
- Stourhead Grotto

In an area bounded by the Severn Estuary in the west, the upper reaches of the Thames in the east, the Cotswolds to the north and the Cheviots to the south, of the eight regions covered by this book, the South Midland region is possibly the most varied of all, containing as it does a wide selection of caves, caverns, mines, tunnels and grottoes. Caves are the foundations of our knowledge of the human race. Early man lived in caves during the Ice Age and it is from the remains of his long dead fires, domestic garbage tips and work areas, that we have derived our tentative knowledge of the people who populated Britain thousands of years before the world's first pictographs formed a basis for written human history.

Of all the numerous caves in the land which have at one time or another provided shelter for primitive man, those at Cheddar and Wookey are the best known. Situated a convenient distance from the M5 they are, perhaps,

Continued overleaf

amongst the best locations for the would-be speleologist to begin to study the geological formation, flora and fauna of caves. While human remains have been found in plenty at both these sites, those with a penchant for tombs would do better to explore the picturesque soft rolling hills of the south Cotswolds. Gloucestershire is littered with round barrows, the circular mounds of earth thrown up over Bronze Age burials or cremations. But it is the Neolithic long barrows that archeologists find so fascinating. The list includes Notgrove, Nympsfield, Windmill Tump and West Kennet, which is near the mysterious Silbury Hill, the largest artificial mound in Europe. We have included two, Belas Knap and Uley, also known by the delightful name of Hetty Pegler's Tump.

Referred to in the *Daily Sketch* for 23rd of November 1943 as

'. . . a secret city under green fields, a vast subterranean ammunition dump, invisible and bomb-proof, hundreds of feet below ground, holding millions of rounds of ammunition . . . with railway stations, canteens, air-conditioned barrack rooms . . . a power house, telephone exchange and 14 miles of conveyor belts . . .'

Monkton Farleigh is almost beyond comprehension. The ingenuity and skill required to convert this one-time underground stone quarry, dating back to the Roman Occupation, into a secret eighty-acre Central Ammunition Depot during the brief prelude to the Second World War, defies imagination.

On a totally different scale, but no less short on ingenuity, are the coal and ironstone mines scattered throughout the leafy Forest of Dean. It is a good idea to make your first port of call the comprehensive Dean Heritage Centre to be found between Cinderford and Blakeney. There is a lot to see in this compact but largely overlooked area which teems with interest for anyone keen on industrial archeology. The forest is also a delightful place for a picnic or a ramble and who knows, you might just chance upon a Free Miner's private drift mine.

There are, unfortunately, few grottoes of any note. However, the grotto at Stourhead is well worth a visit, as is the charming Palladian house built for the merchant banker Henry Hoare. The lakes and gardens are perfectly charming, particularly in the spring when the many exotic and ornamental trees can be seen at their best.

Belas Knap

Belas Knap stands above the 950 feet (290 metre) contour on the top of the hill above Humblebee How plantation, near the western edge of the Cotswold Hills, beyond the eastern edge of Cleeve Common. It is quite a long, steep climb from the road, but once clear of the woods, the footpath offers spectacular views over Winchcombe and the surrounding countryside. A fine example of a Neolithic long barrow, its curvilinear teardrop form measures approximately 178 feet (54 metres) long, 60 feet (18 metres) wide and 13 feet (4 metres) high. Perhaps to fool grave robbers, the people who built it provided a splendid false portal at the north end, framed with large limestone jambs and lintels set in a forecourt flanked by projecting dry-stone revetments.

The original mound was evidently carefully constructed from oolitic limestone blocks bounded by a dry wall of thin Cotswold slates. There are a total of four burial chambers, two in opposite sides near the middle, one at the south-east angle and one at the narrower south end. Those are formed by upright slabs linked by dry walling and were originally covered by corbelled roofs. They contained the remains of some thirty-eight human skeletons together with animal bones, flint instruments and pottery typical of the end of the New Stone Age, *circa* 2000 BC. After burial the passages leading to the chambers were roughly blocked with stones and clay. The lintels and much of the dry-stone walling were rebuilt on the lines of the original between 1863 and 1865 when the barrow was first explored. Between 1928 and 1931 the walling was secured and the chambers covered and the contour of the mound restored as authentically as possible.

It seems a sad reflection on the current collective attitude to Britain's irreplaceable heritage that, after remaining intact over a span of some 5,000 years, the stone blocking the false north portal should be cracked by revellers lighting a barbecue fire against it. Silent and slumbering, doing no one any harm, an out-of-the-way barrow is naturally vulnerable, nevertheless one cannot help wondering how its ancient inhabitants might have reacted, had they been able.

General Information

Owner: Department of the Environment
Title: Belas Knap Long Barrow
Location: 2 miles (3 kilometres) south of Winchcombe near Charlton Abbots, Gloucestershire. Map reference OS sheet 163 SP 021254, Hailes Abbey OS sheet 150 SP 050300
Enquiries: English Heritage at Hailes Abbey, near Winchcombe, Cheltenham, Gloucestershire
Telephone: 0242 602398
Directions: For Belas Knap follow the signs. Steep footpath through wood to field path. Follow field path through two wicket gates.
Access: Any reasonable time. The information/sales point at Hailes Abbey is open daily April to September, 9.30 a.m.–6.30 p.m., in winter it is closed Tuesday, Wednesday and Thursday. (Note: English Heritage opening times are currently under review.)
Nearest car park: There is a small lay-by at the foot of Humblebee How plantation.
Distance: Just over half a mile (one kilometre)
Time to explore: Allow one hour
Conditions: The access path is steep and can be muddy in wet weather. Sensible shoes are advised.
Facilities: None, but further information can be obtained from the English Heritage kiosk at Hailes Abbey, 2 miles north-east of Winchcombe, off 146, where there is a small bookshop and lavatories including facilities for the disabled.

Clearwell Caves

Clearwell Caves are situated in an area of outstanding natural beauty at the centre of a mining region where iron has been extracted for some 2,500 years. The eight caverns open to the public are a mere fraction of a complex which extends over some 600 acres (245 hectares) and consists of literally thousands of caverns connected by countless miles of tunnel and passageway. The caves themselves are part of a natural cave system gradually eroded from the crease limestone of the area. Because the locality was particularly rich in iron and coal, chemical combination caused the groundwater to be particularly acidic. This solution, washing through the caves over many thousands of years and carrying with it dissolved iron, resulted in a rich coating of the various ores of the metal being deposited on the cave walls. It is said that to break into a cavern full of these ores was a visually breathtaking experience as the stalactites of the purple, red, brown and yellow hematites were encrusted with crystals of sparkling calcite.

Visitors to the caves follow the track of a two-foot gauge tramway which descends steeply into the depths of the mine. To the left and right side chambers open up at different levels as the underground vista unfolds. One passes pools made by the miners as a source of drinking water, through chambers where horseshoe and long-eared bats hibernate in winter, to the deepest part of the mine open to the public at 108 feet (33 metres). The limestone dips from west to east at an angle of approximately fifteen degrees which is why the passageways of the mine zigzag up and down the strata so bewilderingly. The impression is of being much deeper, but here in reality the visitor is barely a sixth of the way down. Clearwell was eventually mined to a depth of 650 feet (200 metres) below the surface, but when the mine closed and pumping ceased, the water-table returned to its normal level of about 425 feet (130 metres).

It is now that the visitor can appreciate the effort required to take the ore up to the surface. Traditionally women and children were employed to do this work, carrying 66 pounds (30

Continued overleaf

kilogrammes) at a time – until the law of 1842 prohibited them working in mines. Meanwhile their menfolk laboured at the working face with a stick clenched between their teeth to which a candle was glued with a lump of clay. This primitive personal candelabra was referred to locally as a 'Nelly'.

Back on the surface if time permits it is a good idea to repair to the cosy 'Miners' Canteen'. Located in a conspicuous squat four-square building which was once an engine house, with its welcoming log fire it is the perfect place to relax after a trip underground. Appropriately the Wrights have furnished the room with chairs and tables, most of which once graced the parlours and kitchens of local miners' cottages. Together with the mining pictures and artefacts these strengthen links with the past, making it all the more conducive to sit over a cup of tea and a slice of homemade cake and ponder on the lives of the Forest of Dean Free Miners, their customs, laws and peculiar vocabulary.

As holders of a large proportion of the mining rights of the Forest of Dean limestone basin, Clearwell Caves can arrange extended underground tours for anyone with a serious interest in iron mining, cave formations, geology or local industrial archeology. The area covered is some 1.8 miles (3 kilometres) by 0.6 miles (1 kilometre) and anyone who is fit can volunteer, always provided they are prepared to crawl through the odd narrow access hole or descend pipe-shafts connecting the various sections.

General Information

Owner: Ray and Jonathan Wright
Title: Clearwell Caves Ancient Iron Mines
Location: Clearwell, Near Coleford, Royal Forest of Dean, Gloucestershire
Enquiries: Clearwell Caves
Telephone: 0594 23700
Directions: From Coleford take the B4228 to Lydney and follow the signs, turning right at the Lambsquay Hotel.
Access: Open daily, including Sundays, March to October and 1st to 24th December, 10 a.m.–5 p.m.
Nearest car park: Ample free car/coach parking on site
Distance: 100 metres
Time to explore: Self-guided tours half an hour. Guided tours one hour. Deep level trips two hours minimum.
Conditions: Dry, well graded footpaths throughout. The caves are suitable for the more adventurous disabled.
Facilities: Small gift shop specializing in books on the mining and geology of the area; picnic area, tea room, restaurant; lavatories. Display of early pictures, photographs and documents relating to local mining. Collection of miners' lamps and hand tools. Deep level tours by prior arrangement for groups up to ten.
Parties: School and coach parties welcome.

Dean Heritage Centre

The Dean Heritage Centre was created at Camp Mill to interpret the unique heritage of the Forest of Dean. The mill has its own history spanning nigh on 400 years – from iron foundry to piggery. When the Dean Heritage Museum Trust took the site over in 1981, the main buildings were derelict and the now tranquil mill pond was a scrapyard. But thanks to the far-sightedness of the Trust and with a lot of help from its 'Friends', the supportive body who provide practical assistance in the perennial job of preserving and interpreting the forest heritage, the complex has been made into one of the wonders of Wyedean.

The beauty of the museum is that it is situated smack in the heart of this once massively important industrial area. No matter whether the visitor is a keen industrial archeologist or someone out to enjoy the peculiar tranquility to be found in this ancient Royal Forest, everything is on the doorstep, literally. In the museum you will find a graphic account of the privileges and powers available to a young man born within the Hundred of St Briavels once he became a member of the Free Mining fraternity. It shows how the woodlands supplied the miner and his family with most of their needs – common land where they could graze their sheep, acorns for the pig, bracken to burn to 'lye' for softening water, wild fruit and berries. There is a wooden relief model showing the mine workings and main coal seams of the forest and finally a reconstruction of a typical 'Free Mine' showing techniques that were in use in pre-Roman times and which are employed by the few local Free Miners who still ply a crafty pick-axe around the forest today.

The free-mining rights of the Forest of Dean are set down in a document which stipulates the Dean Miners' own unique codes of practice known as 'Laws and Privileges', sometimes referred to locally as the 'Book of Dennis'. This states that only a man twenty-one years or over who was born within the Hundred of St Briavals, has a free-mining father and has worked for a year and a day in a mine located in the same Hundred, is eligible to become a Free Miner. If he is accepted, theoretically he can establish his 'Gale' – the area in which he decides to dig for coal or iron – anywhere he may choose, apart from consecrated ground or in an orchard bearing fruit. Interpreted literally this meant that there was effectively nothing to stop a Free Miner commencing mining activities more or less anywhere. Up until the mid-eighteenth century such a miner had the swingeing powers of the Dean Free Miners' Court of Mine Law to back him up in the event of any dispute. The problems of living with such a law can well be imagined.

In the past the Forest of Dean has tended to sadly neglect its industrial and social history. Once the cradle of British iron making, sited on the banks of the navigable River Severn and blessed with what at one time must have appeared to be inexhaustible local supplies of wood for charcoal burning, iron ore and coal, its future must once have seemed assured for all time. The origin of Dean iron mining and making is uncertain, but it is known that the industry had been established for several hundred years before the Romans arrived. Initially the miners worked the outcrops; ancient 'Scowles' can still be seen amongst the woods of yew and beech. But as demand grew, they were forced to dig deeper. However, their problems really started when the old fashioned smelting techniques were overtaken by the invention of the blast furnace.

Their staple fuel was charcoal and, so hungry were the enthusiastic iron workers for the material that they completely disregarded the fact that by destroying the woodlands they were ultimately destroying their livelihood. In those days it wasn't the ozone layer or acid rain that concerned the charcoal burners, it was the King. In 1674 Charles II and Parliament acted against the greedy local ironmen and ordered the ironworks demolished in order to save the forest. And that was the end of that – until the nineteenth century and the arrival of the coke-fuelled blast furnace. Suddenly coal was in great demand. This too took its toll on a forest which had barely recovered from the depredations of the charcoal burners. The Free Miners wanted pit props and claimed the right to take timber free of charge. Backed by the Court of Mine Law and the Constable of St Briavels Castle who administered it, they were all but inviolate. Eventually the Crown again prevailed, but the writing was on the wall for the independent miners anyway. Soon big business and outside money choked Free Miners almost out of existence. And then, in turn, lack of profitability killed big business too. Now for the most part only the history, the ruins and the legends remain.

General Information

Owner: Dean Heritage Museum Trust
Title: Dean Heritage Centre
Location: Camp Mill, Soudley, Cinderford, Gloucestershire
Enquiries: The Heritage Centre office
Telephone: 0594 22170
Directions: Camp Mill is on the B4227 between Cinderford and the A48 at Blakeney.
Access: Open daily all year except Christmas Day and Boxing Day. April to October 10 a.m.–6 p.m., November to March 10 a.m.–5 p.m.
Nearest car park: Ample free car/coach parking on site
Distance: 55 yards (50 metres)
Time to explore: One hour minimum, two or three hours for the whole complex
Conditions: Centrally heated museum. There are short ramps easily negotiated by wheelchair.
Facilities: Picnic area with barbecue hearths, restaurant and snack-bar, lavatories including facilities for handicapped persons. Craft shop and gallery selling a wide range of unusual hand-crafted goods and souvenirs. Forest Ranger service, nature trails, guided tours and walks. Adventure play area. Working craftsmen. Living forest exhibition. Displays of

Continued overleaf

charcoal burning and woodcrafts, forest smallholding, observation beehive, wood ant formicarium, agricultural implements, craftsmen's tools, beam engine and water-wheel. There is a level Nature Trail suitable for wheelchairs.

Parties: School and coach parties are welcome. The restaurant caters for parties by arrangement. Organizers are requested to make all group bookings in advance by contacting the Heritage Centre. If writing please enclose a s.a.e.

Gough's Cave

Cheddar Gorge has been rated one of the wonders of England since before Magna Carta. Certainly there are few other places in Britain to match the claustrophobic grandeur of this sheer-sided canyon, carved out of the limestone during countless Ice Age summers by an ancient ancestor of the present-day Cheddar Yeo River. Twisting and turning its way down the primeval Mendip Hills towards Bradley Cross, over the millennia the torrent cut its way into the rock to a depth of over 450 feet (140 metres), dissolving the limestone and scooping out caves and caverns, before disappearing below ground to become one of the largest subterranean water-course systems in the country.

Although Cox's Cave was the first of the Cheddar Caves to be opened to the public, Gough's is the more pre-eminent of the two. As synonymous with Cheddar as Cheddar is with cheese, Gough's has everything you could wish for in a show cave in spectacular abundance; perhaps this fact was not altogether lost on the more perspicacious cave dwellers of the past as it is known to have been inhabited intermittently by man, and of course woman, since the end of the Ice Age some 12,000 years ago.

From the numerous flint and bone tools found during excavation of the cave's earth floor, the first to live there were hunters of the Upper Palaeolithic period who adopted the more accessible local caves for their winter quarters. Many of the artefacts these people left behind are on display in the Cave Museum. Here you will also come face-to-face with the famous Cheddar man, whose remains were discovered in 1903 near the cave mouth, giving rise to the theory that Gough's was once used by our Mesolithic ancestors as catacombs for ritual internment. He is thought to have been about twenty-three years of age at the time of his death which radio-carbon dating indicates

took place some 9,000 years ago, suggesting that he was, culturally speaking, Creswellian.

Gough's Cave owes its discovery to a retired sea captain, Richard Cox Gough, the nephew of the owner of Cox's Cave. Bent on finding a cavern that he could open to the public, and having already blasted his way into a small cave higher up the cliff, in 1890, at the age of sixty-three, he began extending a more promising opening lower down. It took him and his two sons eight years energetic digging before they were able to break through the congealed clay and cave earth into the magnificent Chambers christened St Paul's and Diamond. Such was his pride and enthusiasm that, it is said, within the hour Gough had marshalled his entire family into the former, and amidst the underground splendours of his latest discovery, led them in singing *Praise God from whom all blessings flow*.

Since Gough's time, much has been done to make his cave more easily accessible to the public, including blasting a 40 metre long tunnel to improve the visual amenities. But, as yet, nothing has been revealed to surpass the flowstone sculptures of the Diamond Chamber, some of which have been well over half-a-million years in forming: Archangel's Wing, Solomon's Temple, Organ Pipes and Niagara Falls, all skillfully lit to perfection and cleaned down regularly with steam and dilute hydrochloric acid.

In addition to the normal route, more adventurous visitors are encouraged to join the regular Adventure Caving Expeditions. Kitted out with boiler suits, helmets and miners' lamps, members of the public are taken by their guide beyond the limits of mains lighting and concrete footpaths. The only proviso is that they do not attempt to break the feat of endurance set by one intrepid caver who recently

Continued on page 73

The crease limestone caverns at Clearwell dip at
fifteen degrees and were once richly encrusted with
brightly coloured deposits of iron-oxide. (page 65)

Left
Visitors to underground Britain will find this exotic cluster of stalagmites known as the 'Transformation Scene' in Cox's Cave, the oldest of the Cheddar caves presently open to the public (page 63)

Above
Just part of the fourteen miles of conveyor belts that handled the largest concentration of TNT in Europe at the once very hush, hush Monkton Farleigh 'ammo' dump (page 74)

Spot lights cut through the perennial haze of the
'Witch's Kitchen' highlighting the silent River Axe in
the first of Wookey Hole's numerous chambers (page 76)

spent 113 days and nights on his own, putting both himself and the cave into the *Guinness Book of Records*.

The frontiers of exploration have now progressed far beyond the area of the cave seen by the public. Like Wookey, Gaping Gill and countless other natural caves, Gough's is part of a huge underground system, the total extent of which will almost certainly never be fully explored. By the summer of 1988 two intrepid adventurers had managed to reach a point some 550 yards (500 metres) beyond the limits of the mother cave and more than 115 feet (35 metres) below sea level, in what experts now consider is the most dangerous cave system presently being explored in the British Isles. They were unable to proceed further because the current was too strong to swim against, but no doubt someone will find a way.

General Information

Owner: Longleat Enterprises
Title: Cheddar Caves
Location: Cheddar, Somerset
Enquiries: Cheddar Caves office
Telephone: 0934 742343
Directions: Cheddar Gorge is situated on the B3135
Access: Open daily all year, except Christmas, 10 a.m.–5.30 p.m. in summer and 11 a.m.–4.30 p.m. during winter months. Adventure caving expeditions on most days throughout the year
Nearest car park: Ample car/coach parking nearby
Distance: 110 yards (100 metres)
Time to explore: One hour or two hours for the whole complex
Conditions: Excellent concrete footpaths throughout permit easy access for wheelchairs which are allowed in free. There are flights of steps in the further reaches of the caves.
Facilities: Cafeteria and snack bar. Gift shop selling a wide range of souvenirs. Museum and Exhibition showing many artefacts found in the caves. A 16 mm colour film and video of the caves is available on free loan to schools, coach operators, groups and organizations. There is a nearby licensed restaurant. Guided adventure caving expeditions – hard hats, lamps and boiler suits provided.
Parties: School and coach parties welcome.

Hetty Pegler's Tump

Hetty Pegler's Tump is a Neolithic communal burial mound situated on the top of a steep beech-wood-covered escarpment on the western edge of the Cotswold Hills, overlooking the Severn Valley, in the parish of Uley between Dursley and Nailsworth. Its curious name derives from the former owners of the field in the late seventeenth century, Henry Pegler and his wife Hester.

The tumulus is one of a member of the Severn-Cotswold group of chambered long barrows dating from 3000 to 1800 BC. The 120 feet (36.5 metres) long earth mound covers a cairn of oolitic slabs edged with dry-stone walling. The entrance portal is thought to be a nineteenth century reconstruction and leads to a 22 feet (76.7 metres) long gallery of large upright stones infilled with dry stone. Although the entrance is barely crouching height, the passageway itself is over 3 feet (1 metre) wide and about 5 feet (1.5 metres) high. There were originally two pairs of transepts or side chambers and an end chamber formed by the continuation of the gallery, but the barrow was pillaged in the early nineteenth century by stone-diggers and the two northern chambers damaged beyond repair.

It is impossible to say how much of the structure is original as the barrow was opened in 1821 and subsequently suffered 'restoration' on at least three separate occasions. During the dig of 1821 a total of fifteen human skeletons were found and again in 1854 a further eight were found. In addition to Neolithic remains, there was also evidence that the mound had been used for intrusive internment during the Roman period, as a skeleton, coins and fragments of Roman pottery were also discovered in 1821.

Like Belas Knap, Hetty Pegler's Tump is a silent place, although more easily accessible, being visible from the nearby road. As are the gliders which, on a breezy day, can be seen crabbing along the line of the steep west-facing escarpment in an attempt to make their flight from nearby Nympsfield last as long as possible.

Continued overleaf

General Information

Owner: The Department of the Environment
Title: Uley Long Barrow (Hetty Pegler's Tump)
Location: 3.5 miles (5.5 kilometres) north-east of Dursley, 8 miles (13 kilometres) from Stroud on the B4066 in Gloucestershire. Map reference OS sheet 162, SO 790000. Hailes Abbey OS sheet 150 SP 050300
Enquiries: English Heritage at Hailes Abbey, near Winchcombe, Cheltenham, Gloucestershire
Telephone: 0242 602398
Directions: Sign-posted Uley Tumulus from B4066 Eastington/Nymphsfield junction.

Access: Any reasonable time. The information/sales point at Hailes Abbey is open daily April to September 9.30 a.m.–6.30 p.m.; in winter it is closed Tuesday, Wednesday and Thursday. (Note: English Heritage opening times are currently under review.)
Nearest car park: None
Distance: 440 yards (400 metres) from road
Time to explore: Half an hour
Conditions: The access footpath crosses a field and can be muddy in wet weather. Sensible shoes are advised.
Facilities: None. Further information can be obtained from the English Heritage kiosk at Hailes Abbey, 2 miles north-east of Winchcombe off A46, where there is a small bookshop and lavatories including facilities for the disabled.

Monkton Farleigh Mine

Monkton Farleigh was once one of the most top secret military establishments in Britain. An amazing eighty-acre, bomb-proof arsenal, it makes most other similar installations pale in comparison. First worked for Bath Stone in 1752, Monkton Farleigh Mine was destined to become Europe's largest World War Two underground ammunition depot. Conversion to an MOD storage facility began as late as 1938 during the build up of international tension immediately preceding the outbreak of hostilities. Over 7,500 labourers were brought in to help the army personnel employed and between them they ultimately created a stone, concrete and brick labyrinth capable of storing over 165,000 tons of high explosive. Money was no object. A vast subterranean 'city' was created, served by a conveyor tunnel over a mile long, built to replace the 1.75 mile (2.8 kilometre) long ropeway connecting the store with the main line railway at a secret underground marshalling yard; the transporting of high explosives in broad daylight being considered too dangerous to risk.

Other, calculated risks were taken however. Time being of the essence, the fact that the depot was in full use did not prevent new tunnels being blasted out of solid rock within a stone's throw of enough high explosive to put Bath into orbit! The fact that this work was carried out during the Dunkirk emergency, when large quantities of ammunition had to be stored wherever possible, may have influenced such an apparently foolhardy decision.

But perhaps some inkling of the sheer scale of these excavations can be had when one considers that the air conditioning plant alone cost over a quarter of a million pounds way back in 1943, and the cost of running the 25,000 odd light bulbs twenty-four hours a day does not bear thinking about! Ventilated by eight enormous axial flow blowers which whirred young hurricanes of warm, dry air through the maze of passages and with an arterial system of high-speed conveyors and narrow-gauge railways, the installation needed its own emergency marine-engined generating set. Working in conjunction with a magnificent museum-piece of a switch-room, the giant dynamo could take over in the event of a mains power failure so that the vital job of loading and off-loading ammunition could go on around the clock. Sadly scrap merchants ripped out most of the copper wiring when the MOD left, but the thirsty old diesel engine is in place and said to be still operational.

It is difficult to adequately describe the enormity of this man-made underground monument to the tax payer, it simply has to be seen to be believed. Yet incongruously, above the surface there is very little to see. A few queer-looking derelict barns dotted about Farleigh Rise are the only indication that 100 feet (30 metres) below the hilltop was once Britain's biggest 'ammo' dump. In its heyday it would have been throbbing with noise and activity, but now it is as silent as the grave. It would be a very intrepid trespasser indeed who ventured into the echoing depths without a qualified guide – they could still be trying to find the exit by the time Star-wars have become a reality.

General Information

Owners: Monkton Farleigh Mine Ltd
Title: Monkton Farleigh Mine
Location: Farleigh Rise, Monkton Farleigh, Wiltshire. Map reference OS sheet 804651
Enquiries: Monkton Farleigh Mine Ltd
Telephone: 0225 852400
Directions: Take the A4 from Bath for Chippenham and after approximately 4 miles (6.4 kilometres) turn right onto the A363 for Bradford-upon-Avon. At Pinckney Green turn left to Monkton Farleigh.

Access: Open daily from Easter to October from 11 a.m. Last tour at 4 p.m. Winter season open Saturdays and Sundays only.
Nearest car park: Large free car/coach park on site
Distance: 55 yards (50 metres)
Time to explore: One and a half hours
Conditions: Dry asphalt floors throughout. There is a steep 100 feet (30 metre) access ramp down to the mine.
Facilities: Picnic area; light refreshments, hot and cold drinks; lavatories. Small gift shop selling war memorabilia. Hourly guided tours. Small aircraft and military vehicle museum. Public footpath to Brown's Folly Nature Reserve which offers fine views over the Avon towards Bath.
Parties: School and coach parties welcome.

Stourhead Grotto

Stourhead was designed by Colen Campbell for Henry Hoare the first, the wealthy merchant banker, son of the founder of Hoare's Bank, who bought the estate in 1717. Completed in 1720, it was one of the first houses in Britain to be built in the refreshingly new Palladian style. Unfortunately the central block was gutted by fire in 1902 and was painstakingly restored as an exact copy of the original. The gardens were started by Henry Colt Hoare in 1740 and represent a definitive example of eighteenth-century English gardening philosophy, derived from the paintings produced by the contemporary French landscape artists such as Claude who were enjoying considerable favour at the time. Notable for their allusions of the poetic and the abstract, such pictures were responsible for the fashionable move away from the pernickety formal layouts popular during the proceeding century, the origins of which went right back to the Elizabethan era, and they established a style which culminated in the great sweeping informal parklands of Capability Brown.

In abandoning formal patterns, Hoare was well ahead of his time and very much breaking new ground; Brown did not set himself up as a landscape consultant until 1749 and it was not until well into the second half of the century that his work began to reach fruition. The pivotal point of the gardens at Stourhead is the irregularly shaped lake which was formed by the simple expedient of damming a small stream running through the grounds. Set amongst the folds of the surrounding hills which Hoare had densely planted with fir and beech, are sinuous pathways which present ever-changing vistas of leafy glades containing rare trees and punctuated by classical temples whose dignified architecture is reflected in the still waters of the ornamental lake. To modern eyes, delightful though they are, Hoare's gardens do not appear particularly unconventional, yet, of course, to the formalists, in their day, they were revolutionary, and to add insult to injury they even boasted a grotto. One can almost hear the sharp intake of breath!

Grottoes had a classical pedigree and were essentially reintroduced into Italian Renaissance gardens to provide cool shade and sometimes an unexpected shower-bath for the unwary, if the owner happened to possess a sense of humour; hardly becoming behaviour in the English climate. But the eighteenth-century penchant for the 'Grand Tour' naturally brought them to notice and Georgian enthusiasm for novelty did the rest. While to us the grotto may look dark, damp and unappealing, to the avant-garde of the period they evidently aroused subconscious primeval urges. Besides providing the feeling of sanctuary common to a cave, they could also be exploited as a romantic home for nymphs and ogres. Usually

Continued overleaf

these were merely stone carvings, although some enthusiastic proprietors actually went as far as to commission their own tame hermit to take up residence and go 'boo' at the appropriate time when visitors chanced by. Some of these wild men of the woods were even encouraged to talk to their aristocratic guests, in a suitably bucolic manner.

Stourhead, as far as we know, never had a hermit. Nor did it originally have azaleas, hydrangeas or rhododendrons; they were planted in the nineteenth century. However it does have a particularly pleasing grotto, approached by way of a dark walk through the trees made more memorable by brief glimpses of the mirrored waters of the lake. An arched passage leads into the principal room which is circular and about 20 feet (6 metres) in diameter, from which there are yet more views of the lake and a recess in which a drowsy nymph reclines over a little cascade. A second arched passage leads to Stour's Cave where a petrified ogre holds an urn from which he permanently pours icy crystal-clear spring water. The statues are by Cheere, the setting is superb and the overall effect wholly delightful.

General Information

Owner: The National Trust
Title: Stourhead Grotto
Location: Stourhead, Stourton, Warminster, Wiltshire
Enquiries: The National Trust Visitor Centre, Stourhead
Telephone: 0747 840348
Directions: Stourhead is 3 miles (4.8 kilometres) north-west of Mere off the B3092
Access: Garden: daily 8 a.m.–7 p.m. or sunset; house: April and October, Saturday to Wednesday 2 p.m.–6 p.m., May to September, daily except Friday, 2 p.m.–6 p.m.
Nearest car park: Ample free car/coach parking on site
Distance: 275 yards (250 metres)
Time to explore: House: one hour minimum; gardens: two hours minimum.
Conditions: Graded footpaths and lawns. The path around the lake is 1.5 miles (2.5 kilometres) and is ideal for wheelchairs. There are 13 steps up to the house which is unsuitable for wheelchairs.
Facilities: The nearby Spread Eagle Inn at the garden entrance is open all the year round, has a restaurant and provides bar snacks. There are picnic areas and lavatories including facilities for handicapped persons.
Parties: School and coach parties welcome.

Wookey Hole

Long before the troubadours thought fit to embroider the perennial Arthurian legends of the mysterious Vale of Avelon with stories of cave dwelling witches and lakeland ladies, Mendip was covered by warm, shallow seas full of tiny calcarious sea creatures. In time their remains were compressed into the rock we now call carboniferous limestone. Then, when the Earth's crust was squeezed, some 270 million years ago, the area around Wookey was forced into a mountainous arch a mile high. Natural erosion gradually wore down the topmost peaks, spreading debris all around and reducing the mountains to mere hills. It was in the foothills of dolomitic conglomerate resulting from this process that the effects of a million years of rain and successive Ice Ages produced the extensive cave system to which Wookey Hole belongs.

Folklore is an abstruse subject and frequently the origin of a particular myth or fable is lost in the dim recesses of time. So it is with the legendary Witch of Wookey. She probably meant little to the early Stone Age people hunting bear and rhinoceros who first used the caves as a winter shelter as long as 50,000 years ago. Certainly the superstitious Celts who, much later, evidently found Wookey a safe and relatively comfortable place to live, could not have been unduly worried by the mysterious shadows cast by their flickering fires. So it is Christian culture and its preoccupation with the ancient Judaic concepts of 'good' and 'evil' to which we have to turn for the source of the tale.

The most well-known version concerns a wizened old woman, living alone with her dog in the shadowy fastness of the caves, who spent her time casting spells on the villagers and their cattle, turning the milk sour, and who was, in effect, the scapegoat for every local mishap and calamity. Instead of trying to make friends, the people of Wookey summoned a monk from nearby Glastonbury to exorcise her. One day when she was busy casseroling a child, she was-confronted by the monk and fled into the gloom of the inner cavern now known as the Witch's Kitchen. With great presence of mind the monk scooped up some water from the sub-terranean River Axe, blessed it, and scattered it over the witch and her unfortunate dog, pet-rifying them on the spot into weirdly shaped stalagmites. Legend or not, intriguingly enough, in 1912, the archeologist Herbert Balch found human bones, a dagger and an alabaster ball among Iron Age remains. Balch was not the first to find human remains in the caves of Wookey, however. In 1859, the year Charles Darwin published *On the Origin of Species*, the pioneer archeologist William Boyd Dawkins, a contemporary of William Pengelly, concluded that the mingling of human remains and artefacts with the bones of rhinoceros and woolly mammoth suggested that the human race was at least as old as these extinct animals.

The caves are also a famous venue for the dangerous sport of cave diving which had its beginnings at Wookey, where breathing ap-paratus was used for the first time in 1935. For cave divers the green, clear, Mendip water offered a great challenge and as successive ex-plorers pushed on further into the labyrinth of sumps and submerged tunnels, it became clear that the three chambers seen by the public were but a fraction of the whole system. Cave divers are still very active at Wookey Hole and are constantly probing the unexplored under-ground watercourse of the River Axe. In 1985 a local diver, Robert Parker, diving beyond the limits of Chamber 25, achieved a British record dive of 220 feet (67 metres).

In an effort to let visitors see something of what lay beyond the limits of Chamber 3, in 1974 an artificial tunnel was blasted through the rock to link the 100 feet (33 metre) high Chamber 9 with the outside world. This not only greatly increased the overall length of the tour, but provides those who have sampled the mysteries of the caves with a pleasant walk beside the mill leat which supplies water to the splendid nineteenth-century paper mill, form-ing part of the tour. The mill was the pride and joy of one William Hodgkinson, a stationer, who in 1848 rebuilt the old rundown mill in the best traditions of Victorian architecture in order to specialize in the production of high quality paper for bank notes and legal docu-ments. Visitors can still watch the ancient craft of papermaking practised as it has been for cen-turies in what is now Britain's last handmade paper mill.

But papermaking is not all the mill has in store. Rescued for the second time in its history by none other than Madame Tussauds, it is appropriate that there should be a detailed re-construction of the famous Chamber of Curi-osities, Madame Tussaud's original travelling wax museum, on display. There is also a spec-tacular collection of fairground memorabilia from the days when giant traction engines hauled the travelling fairs with their sideshows and musical rides all over the country. Finally there is an elegant Edwardian Penny Pier Arcade and an absorbing museum with sec-tions depicting the history of the caves, local geology, archeology, cave diving and, of course, the myths and legends. As for the wicked witch and her small dog, she certainly can't be lonely anymore, and with so much going on she surely has no time to be crotchety.

General Information

Owner: Wookey Hole Caves Ltd
Title: Wookey Hole Caves and Mill
Location: Wookey Hole Mill, Wookey Hole, Wells, Somerset
Enquiries: The General Manager, Wookey Hole Caves Ltd
Telephone: 0749 72243
Directions: Situated some 2 miles (3.2 kilometres) west of Wells from which it is well signposted.
Access: Open daily (except the week before Christmas) 9.30 a.m.–5.30 p.m. in summer, 10.30 a.m.–4.30 p.m. in winter.
Nearest car park: Large free car/coach park on site
Distance: 440 yards (400 metres)
Time to explore: Two hours minimum
Conditions: Although access to the caves is safe and easy, there are several short flights of steps and the roof is low in places. The caves are unsuitable for all but the more adventurous disabled. Visitors in wheelchairs are welcome in the mill.
Facilities: Cafeteria serving drinks, snacks, hot and cold meals; indoor and outdoor picnic areas. Working handmade paper mill, 'Old Penny Pier Arcade', 'The Fairground by Night', 'Madame Tussaud's Cabinet of Curiosities'. Gifts and souvenirs available in the Handmade Paper Shop. Lavatories, including facilities for the disabled, in the main car park.
Parties: School and coach parties welcome. Please contact the Party Organizer.

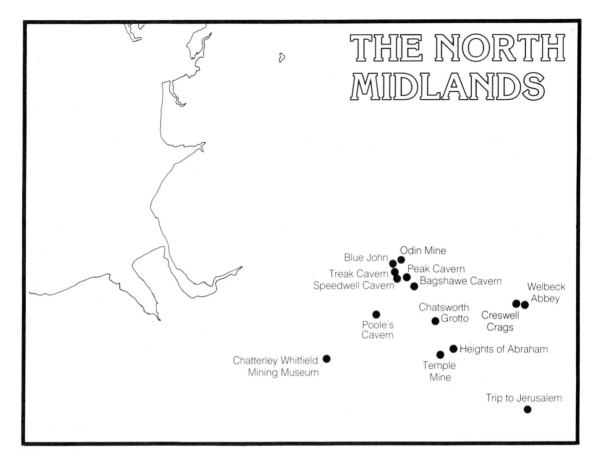

THE NORTH MIDLANDS

Odin Mine
Blue John
Treak Cavern   Peak Cavern
Speedwell Cavern   Bagshawe Cavern
                                        Welbeck
                                        Abbey
                Chatsworth
                    Grotto   Creswell
Poole's   Crags
Cavern

                    Heights of Abraham
Chatterley Whitfield
Mining Museum   Temple
                    Mine

                    Trip to Jerusalem

A glance at the entries for the region we have designated the North Midlands gives the impression that all roads lead to Castleton. In a way they do, for this busy, neat and tidy little village seems to be the gravitational centre of the Peak National Park. Here you will find the tourist-orientated wonders of Blue John, Speedwell, Peak and Treak contrasting noticeably with the informal delights of Bagshawe Cavern at nearby Bradwell.

Snug in a verdant valley on the south-east edge of the Peak District, the walkers' paradise of the North Midlands, Chatsworth needs no introduction. Originally built for the first Duke of Devonshire at the turn of the seventeenth century, with its breathtaking fountains and magnificent gardens, it is without doubt one of the finest country mansions in Britain. The rusticated grotto built during the romantic period some hundred years later has a presence all its own.

It is at Matlock, 25 miles (40 kilometres) south-west of Castleton that another famous centre for caves, caverns and mines is to be found. Dominated by the lead-rich Great Rake vein, according to local tradition, mining has been associated with Matlock and the nearby ancient spa town of Matlock Bath since Roman times. Of the countless mine undertakings that have grown, failed or prospered, several have now opened their doors to visitors. Indeed, Rutland Cavern, now known as Nestus Mine and a part of the Heights of Abraham complex, which, with its cable car access, probably offers the best value for money of all the locations in this book, includes the most famous of all the local caves, Great Masson, which has been a show cave since 1810. Not that it was the first. Cumberland Cavern was opened as early as 1797, but, like a good many others, after being worked as recently as the 1950s, both entrances are now blocked.

Chatterley Whitfield, one of the three mining museums we have included, is an enormous complex which covers almost every aspect of coal mining imaginable. Famous not only for once having the biggest spoil heap in Europe it was also once at the centre of the largest single colliery-created area of derelict land in Europe. The whole site has recently been the subject of a proportionately vast reclamation scheme on the part of Stoke-on-Trent City Council.

Creswell Crags strictly needs a book all to itself. One of the premier pre-historic sites in Europe, if not the world, the careful sifting of bone and fossil fragments from beneath the flowstone deposits in the numerous caves of this unprepossessing limestone gorge have furthered our knowledge of both our cave-dwelling ancestors and the ancient flora and fauna of the locality by an inestimable amount. One of the most important sites in the country for the study of fossils it provides an opportunity to visit a working archeological site of great importance and should not be missed.

Conversely Welbeck College is a location that sadly we must firmly request that you do miss from your itinerary. An army residential college, visiting is not permitted, so please do not ask. It was included purely because the subterranean passages and suites of the fifth Duke of Portland just have to be the most outrageously eccentric underground folly in the whole of the British Isles. Read, learn and believe, if you can.

Those of us who enjoy a tankard of real ale will not wish to miss the historical caves which make up a significant part of the Trip to Jerusalem, an inn that can trace its antecedents back to the Crusades. The nearby Brewhouse Yard Museum and Bridlesmithgate also have ancient caves sculpted out of the Nottingham sandstone.

Bagshawe Cavern

The two small, unpretentious sheds, one stone and one timber, their railings and concrete apron more likely than not festooned with drying water-proofs, look more like temporary headquarters than the well established offices of what is arguably the most different caving experience to be had in the British Isles. But make no mistake, Bagshawe is about as close as the novice can get to potholing without actually joining a regular potholing club. Perhaps the best hint as to what wonders to expect can be deduced from guide Peter Arfield's quietly understated advice to visitors that it is best to wear light outdoor clothes 'you no longer love' if you want to fully enjoy Bagshawe, and wellingtons in the winter or if it has been raining a lot recently. And he was talking about Trip One.

As the leaflet says, there are four distinct types of trip available and they gradually increase in difficulty to cater for all tastes from the casual visitor to the enthusiast. The first of these is perfectly suitable for all the family and takes sightseers down through what used to be an early nineteenth-century lead mine with the quaint name of Mulespinner to the start of the natural cavern system. They are then conducted on an 880 yard (800 metre) tour past festoons of stalactites, stalagmites and flowstone curtains of considerable beauty with descriptive names like Cataract, Chandler's Shop and Grotto of Paradise. Before returning to surface the visitor is taken into an area of natural or 'wild' cave, but for the rudimentary lighting much as it must have looked when the last Ice Age receded. After rain, rivulets of water dampen the boulder-strewn floor giving a taste of what lies beyond. On this trip there are fossils, chimneys, a bedding plain, a pot hole and a floodlit pool to see, but apart from a few brushes with the cave sides – it is distinctly narrow in places – there is nothing untoward to fear, even in the last section.

Trip Two, the adventure trip, is different. Ideal caving for beginners this trip is a perennial favourite with such organizations as

Continued overleaf

Schools, Youth Clubs, Scouts, Guides, Police and Army cadets. It includes chimney climbing, crawling, ladder work, scrambling through an underground river bed and a pot hole, known as the Glory Hole, which is both wet and muddy. For those who like getting wet there is also a simple syphon. An experienced guide accompanies all parties.

Trip Three is only for those who have completed the adventure trip and want to do something a bit harder. Bagshawe has two levels and extends for a known 3,280 yards (3,000 metres) beyond the limits of the concrete path. For the more adventurous there are silent stalactite chambers, large pools to wade through and the by-now-infamous Agony Crawl to negotiate. As a grand finale, and after three hours underground, there is a crawl through a tight squeeze known, appropriately, as Letter Box. This is most definitely not a trip for the portly, it is a trip for the masochistic.

The fourth trip appeals to those interested in speleology or cave photography and visits what are, perhaps, the most unspoiled caves in Derbyshire open to the general public. If you do not mind climbing down the odd 33 feet (10 metre) pot hole there are some beautiful stalactites, helectites and fossils to be seen.

Do ask to read the visitors' book and letters of commendation. The comments speak for themselves: 'The children really enjoyed it, so did we'; 'Makes all other caves a waste of time'; '. . . not a boring minute – great'. We leave the last word to a young convert to caving who signed herself Amanda: 'Magic – lovely and muddy and wet'.

General Information

Owner: Peter Revel
Title: Bagshawe Cavern
Location: Jeffery Lane, Bradwell, Derbyshire. Map reference OS sheet 110 167808
Enquiries: 12 Bradwell Head Road, Bradwell, Sheffield
Telephone: 0433 20540 and 21298
Directions: Bradwell is 2.5 miles, (4 kilometres) from Castleton on the B6049. From the Bowling Green pub take a sharp left into Granby Road, proceed over the crossroads into Jeffrey Lane and Bagshawe is 220 yards (200 metres) on the left.
Access: Open weekends, Easter to May, 2 p.m.–6 p.m. Open daily, June to August, 2 p.m.–6 p.m. Open at other times by prior appointment only.
Nearest car park: Small free car park on site
Distance: 55 yards (50 metres)
Time to explore: From one hour depending on trip
Conditions: Part concrete footpaths, part natural cave; inclined to be wet in places especially during the winter months. There is a flight of about 100 steep steps and the roof is low in places. The cavern is unsuitable for the disabled, the visually handicapped or those suffering from circulatory or respiratory conditions. Stout footwear and old casual clothes are strongly recommended. Protective headgear is provided free. Trips Two, Three and Four all require old clothes, a dry change of clothes and caving/mining lamps.
Facilities: Small shop selling hot and cold drinks, chocolate bars and crisps. A few protective jackets are available if required.
Parties: Small parties are very welcome but strictly by appointment please. Trips Two, Three and Four only by prior booking.

Blue John Cavern

Dominated by the slopes of Mam Tor, the Blue John Cavern is situated in the Peak National Park at the western end of the Hope Valley, near the small town of Castleton. Both the cavern and the surrounding district are of great interest to tourist and geologist alike. While the caverns themselves were formed comparatively recently, albeit a mere 80,000 years ago, by the action of vast quantities of water from melting glacial ice flowing through faults in the carboniferous limestone, the highly prized Blue John, from which the mine gets its name, dates from a much earlier period. Crudely speaking Blue John is nothing more than common or garden fluorspar with sex-appeal. Widely sought after by collectors for its subtle colouration, which can range from the deepest shades of blue-black to amber and even pure white, this chemically impure form of calcium fluoride is only found in workable quantities in Treak Cliff hill.

The reason for the curious purplish-blue bands of colour that distinguish Blue John from blast furnace flux is open to speculation. Geologists now incline to the view that it happened through a highly complex combination of diagenesis and inclusion taking place over millions of years, causing trace-elements and organic compounds to migrate into the fluor-spar, turning this normally transparent mineral into one of the most exquisite of all semi-precious stones to be found in nature's terrestrial paintbox. It is not only scarce, but also difficult to work, since it cracks and fragments very easily. For this reason, perfect specimens are highly prized and rarely seen outside museums or amongst the collections of the discerning.

The guided tour into the cave and mine necessitates climbing down numerous flights of steps to reach the natural part of the system. Look out for the much-prized nodular vein of Blue John as the path descends, twisting and turning through workings and caverns for a considerable distance. Mining of limited quantities of Blue John still continues and various small articles made from the material can be purchased from the souvenir shop.

General Information

Owner: E M and G S Ollerenshaw
Title: Blue John Cavern and Mine
Location: Blue John Cavern and Mine, Castleton, Derbyshire
Enquiries: Blue John Cavern and Mine
Telephone: 0433 20638 or 20642
Directions: Take the Manchester road out of Castleton travelling west. As the lower section of the A625 has been closed due to subsidence, turn left through Winnats Pass. At the top of the pass take first right onto the A625 and follow the yellow signs.
Access: Open daily 9.45 a.m.–5.30 p.m. or dusk except for Christmas Day
Nearest car park: Ample free car/coach parking on site
Distance: 55 yards (50 metres)
Time to explore: 45 minutes
Conditions: Dry, smooth footpaths. There are numerous flights of steps. The cavern is unsuitable for the disabled, the visually handicapped or those suffering from circulatory or respiratory conditions.
Facilities: Gift shop at the entrance specializing in a fine selection of jewellery and ornaments made in Blue John stone. Confectionery, soft drinks and light refreshments are available from the kiosk; lavatories; picnic area.
Parties: School and coach parties welcome.

Chatsworth Grotto

The home of the Duke and Duchess of Devonshire, Chatsworth is one of the grandest country houses in England. Built between 1686 and 1708 for William Cavendish, the first Duke of Devonshire, it was extended in the 1820s to its present form. Extravagantly furnished and decorated throughout, it boasts a magnificent library and world famous collections of porcelain, silver, paintings, drawings and sculpture.

The development of the spectacular gardens was commenced in 1688 when George London created a formal garden in the Derwent valley including the canal and the Neptune fountain. The temple of the famous Grand Cascade by Thomas Archer is of a slightly later date. Capability Brown was commissioned to create an informal 1000 acre (405 hectare) woodland park in his inimitable style, but after the death of the fourth Duke in 1764, the gardens themselves lay relatively undisturbed until Paxton took a hand in 1826. In addition to some monumental conservatories, one of which is said to have been the prototype for his Crystal Palace,

but now, sadly, no longer standing, he was also responsible for the splendid Emperor fountain which throws a jet of water some 290 feet (88 metres) into the air, the highest gravity-fed fountain in the world. Besides the fountain there is a tropical greenhouse, an elaborate rose garden and secluded walks amongst rare shrubs and forest trees. The hydro-electric generating system has recently been restored and works from the same water source as the fountain.

Set in one of the more remote parts of the verdant greenery of this definitive English garden, facing a secluded lake, is the grotto. Designed by White Watson, the Bakewell geologist, it was built in 1798 at a cost of £140 8s 3d. It was later remodelled in 1820 when it was re-roofed, re-floored and lined with mineral specimens from the Ecton copper mine. Constructed from massive sandstone boulders it is set into the hillside, its curved face decorated with geological specimens including stalactites and flowstone carbuncles. Behind the roughly arched entrance is a rectangular

Continued overleaf

room, course-faced with sandstone. On the original plans this was described as the grotto, however, behind a set of massive doors and along a short passage lies the grotto's most interesting feature. Originally described as the 'Mine' there is a circular chamber with evidence of a fireplace. Smoke escaped from this by means of a circular flue within the walls, presumably as an ingenious form of hypocaust to ensure the maximum dissipation of heat. The 'Mine' is surmounted by a rustic summer house formed of eight tree trunks and covered with a conical slate roof.

General Information

Owner: Chatsworth House Trust
Title: Chatsworth Grotto
Location: Chatsworth, Bakewell, Derbyshire. Map reference OS sheet 119 260701
Enquiries: Comptroller, Chatsworth
Telephone: 024688 2204
Directions: Chatsworth is 8 miles (13 kilometres) north of Matlock off the B6012
Access: Open daily, Easter to October, 11.30 a.m.–4.30 p.m.
Nearest car park: Ample free car/coach parking on site
Distance: 110 yards (100 metres)
Time to explore: House: one hour minimum; gardens: two hours minimum
Conditions: Graded gravel footpaths and lawns. The house is unsuitable for wheelchairs.
Facilities: Café; shops; snack bars selling hot and cold drinks, confectionery and ice cream; coach drivers' rest room; lavatories. Camera hire. Audio cassettes available for house tour. Free-loan video for party organizers. House and garden guided tours by arrangement.
Parties: School and coach parties welcome.

Chatterley Whitfield Mining Museum

Coal extraction from the Potteries Coalfield began as early as the late thirteenth century. Initially, as demand developed, the area became dotted with a large number of small pits. As the upper coal measures became exhausted, miners were forced to dig deeper in order to reach productive seams. Thus, while miners working coalfields in more hilly districts were frequently able to take advantage of the topography and drive inclined drifts into out-cropped seams, a comparatively cheap operation, in Staffordshire their only recourse was to sink pits and use machinery to hoist the coal and to drain the mine. It is no accident that the first practical steam engine in the world was erected by Thomas Newcomen at a colliery near Dudley Castle in 1712. But mechanization was expensive and in order to justify the cost it was necessary to increase the coal-producing capacity of the mine. As a result, while Telford was building his canals and bridges and the miners of the Potteries were beavering away below ground, big business was busy taking over the small undertakings and moulding them into viable units.

Evidence suggests that the present Whitfield Colliery has its roots in the middle of the last century. At this time mining on the site was primitive, wasteful and extremely dangerous. The method of working left numerous pillars of coal unmined in order to support the roof and miners ascended and descended in the same crude tubs that were used for hoisting coal. In 1872 the colliery was purchased by the prosperous Chatterley Iron Company but subsequent financial troubles, exacerbated by a disastrous explosion underground in 1881, led to receivers being appointed. The receiver and his son successfully refloated the company and, after an extended programme of improvement, by the early part of the present century had established Chatterley Whitfield as the largest colliery in North Staffordshire.

By 1909 all main hauling roads were lit by electricity, in 1919 the first mechanized coal cutters and shaker conveyors were introduced, and by 1921 the whole pit was using the longwall advancing system of coal working. These and other important innovations enabled Chatterley Whitfield Colliery, in 1937, to be one of the first mines in Britain to produce over 1,000,000 tons (1,016,000 tonnes) of saleable coal in a single year. This figure would be impressive even today, with fully-automated coal handling. It is phenomenal when you consider that the mechanically worked faces were still supported by hand-set pit props. But that million tons becomes a lot more sobering when you discover that, from a total work force of around 4,500 men and boys, that output was won at a cost of something like one dead miner for every 150,000 tons (152,400 tonnes) of coal!

Nationalization came in 1947 and was followed by cheap oil which led to a drop in world coal demand. By 1974 it was decided that coal could be more conveniently worked from nearby Wolstanton Colliery 5 miles (8 kilometres) away, Whitfield being, by then, part of an enormous network of mines. Before it was levelled and recontoured, the Chatterley spoil-heap was by far the largest man-made spoil-heap in Europe. Wolstanton too is now closed, the only operating pits being Holditch, Silverdale, Hem Heath and Florence; still producing some 3,000 tons (3,048 tonnes) per day and having entirely undermined the cities of Stoke-on-Trent and Newcastle-under-Lyme, they are now heading for Stafford.

The story would have ended in 1974 but for the enthusiasm of the men and women who worked and lived in the surrounding area and for which the pit was a way of life. Miners are well known for their determination, and their corporate local desire to preserve something of their heritage and present the story of coal mining through the ages to a wider public resulted in the setting up of the Chatterley Whitfield Mining Museum. Sadly, the closing of Wolstanton resulted in the flooding of Whitfield's deep galleries, but, since first opening to the public in 1979, work has started on a development project to deepen the 'New Pit' and connect it up with the existing Hesketh Shaft. In the meantime there is more than enough to see at this absorbing Museum of Mining.

In the care of ex-miner guides, after being kitted up in the lamp house, visitors are taken underground by way of Platt shaft on an extensive tour through a maze of old workings. Taking a full hour the tour starts in the typical environment of a miner of the 1850s, passes along a low crushed roadway, through a ventilation door into a hand-mined longwall face of the early 1900s. The route continues through a jig dip, a horse level, through a pony stable of the 1920s era and on to a section set out to represent the coal face as it would have been in the mine's hey-day of 1937. An arched and lagged main dip, underground workshops, old roadways and a pump house bring the visitor back to the present day, with an underground man-rider locomotive trip followed by galleries containing examples of the fearsome equipment used down modern mines.

Up top there is much to see so be sure to allow plenty of time for the live steam, an enormous gleaming steam winder, the Pit Canteen and a pony drawing service for the disabled. All are welcome; there are excellent education services for schools and full facilities for the disabled. To describe a visit to Chatterley Whitfield as an 'experience' is tantamount to understatement, 'eye-opener' would be a better term. It should be compulsory for all school children old enough to comprehend just what the term 'coal miner' means.

General Information

Owner: Chatterley Whitfield Mining Museum Trust
Title: Chatterley Whitfield Mining Museum
Location: Tunstall, Stoke-on-Trent, Staffordshire
Enquiries: Visitor Service Officer
Telephone: 0782 813337
Directions: Signposted from Tunstall. The mine is just off the A527 Tunstall to Biddulph/Congleton road.
Access: Open daily, 9 a.m.–5 p.m. Guided tours underground 10 a.m.–4 p.m.
Nearest car park: Ample free car/coach parking on site.
Distance: 110 yards (100 metres)
Time to explore: One hour guided tour, two hours minimum.
Conditions: Dry graded footpaths throughout. Protective headgear and miners' lamps are provided free. Warm clothing and stout footwear are recommended. The mine is unsuitable for the severely disabled but wheelchairs can be admitted with difficulty. Please discuss requirements with the staff in advance.
Facilities: Original 1930s canteen offering refreshments, confectionery and ice cream. Gift shop selling a wide range of books and souvenirs. Lavatories including facilities for handicapped persons. Conference and exhibition rooms. VIP catering service. Working steam and diesel locomotives. Hesketh steam winding engine. Retired pit ponies; working shire horse.
Parties: School and coach parties welcome by arrangement. A free education service is available for school parties. Mobile education road show. Teachers preview tickets.

Creswell Crags

Driving down the narrow, relatively unspectacular grey gorge which is Creswell Crags you might be forgiven for not realizing you are passing through a site of outstanding ancient historical importance. Not just any premier archeological site, but, to quote Professor David Bellamy, '. . . one of the key sites of archeological heritage, not only in Britain, not only in Europe, but in the world'.

The first to stress the importance of Creswell Crags as a site of human occupation was Sir William Boyd Dawkins, a contemporary of the pioneer Cornish palaeontologist William Pengelly (see Kent's Cavern page 43), in 1875–76. The unique historical importance of the site stems from its special link with the last Ice Age when it was occupied at various times by Neanderthal, Modern and finally Creswellian man. The first Neanderthal men came on the scene around 43,000 BC. A subsequent Ice Age drove them to warmer climes, leaving the crags devoid of humans until about 30,000 BC when the glaciers retreated and Modern man took up residence. He was physically more like us and better at fashioning tools than the Neanderthals, but again, after about 3,000 years, the deteriorating climate drove him away leaving the gorge to the bears and hyenas. Then, around 12,000 years ago Creswellian man drove them out and assumed ownership.

Unlike his contemporaries in other parts of Europe, Creswellian man made his mark as a bone carver, not a cave painter. One of the world's earliest and most famous works of art, the head of a horse, delicately engraved on a fragment of rib bone, was discovered in one of the caves hidden amongst the wooded banks of the river, just above flood level at the foot of the crags. There are at least twenty-five such caves there, some little more than fissures in the rock, others substantial caverns, the five major ones being Boat House, Church Hole, Pin Hole, Robin Hood's and Mother Grundy's Parlour.

However, human relics are not the only aspect of importance at Creswell. Over thousands of years, the materials carried into the caves by streams of ground water, together with residue eroded from the roofs, built up on the floor of the caves, to form layers of sands and earths which eventually almost blocked the caves. These accumulations, sealed with magnesian-rich flowstone, have subsequently become the treasure trove of archeologists who, excavating beneath many centuries of stalagmite deposit, have found both animal bones and the bone and stone tools used by early man. But why does that make Creswell so unique and so important? Because the solutions leached out of the magnesian limestone effectively encapsulated these objects in a protective coating which is dateable, preserving a unique time capsule which goes back to the last two Ice Ages and beyond.

At last scientists can interpolate vital information about some of the first people ever to live in Britain and, later, some of the most technically and artistically advanced, and what is more, they can put dates to them. But it does not stop there. By careful analysis it is possible to read the layers of flowstone like a calendar. Petrified pollen grains discovered at Creswell have provided firm evidence of a warm interglacial period 165,000 years ago. The only other places to provide evidence of that sort are the deep sea cores – and all they show is what was then living in the sea, not what was happening on the land. Science has been trying to establish a date for this landscape-changing event for years. It is thanks to the combined enthusiasm of the two County Councils, and the generous support of numerous sponsors, that such things are possible.

General Information

Owner: Derbyshire and Nottinghamshire County Councils
Title: Creswell Crags
Location: Creswell Crags Visitor Centre, Crags Road, Welbeck, near Worksop, Nottinghamshire. Map reference OS sheet 120 537744
Enquiries: Creswell Crags Visitor Centre
Telephone: 0909 720378
Directions: Creswell Crags is on the B6402 (Crags Road) between the A616 and A60, one mile (1.6 kilometres) east of Creswell village.

Access: December to February, Sundays only 10 a.m.–4.30 p.m. March to October, Tuesday to Sunday 10 a.m.–5 p.m. Public access to the caves is prohibited in the interests of safety. There is no charge for admission to the Visitor Centre.
Nearest car park: Ample free car/coach parking on site
Distance: 55 yards (50 metres)
Time to explore: Approximately two hours
Conditions: Smooth, graded footpaths throughout
Facilities: Shop/display well stocked with books, leaflets and slides about Creswell, general interest publications, maps and souvenirs. Picnic area and lavatories. All facilities are suitable for the disabled. Exhibition: 'The Age of Ice', a look back in time covering 80,000 years of change in climate, animals and man. Audio-Visual Show: 'The Reindeer Hunters', a slide show enabling children to understand the way of life of the people who once inhabited the crags. Lakeside Discovery Trail: a pleasant walk around the caves revealing information about past and present life at Creswell Crags. Special activities for schools including: Storytelling Service (5 to 11-year-olds), Stone Age Simulations (11 to 15-year-olds), Lucky Dip – a micro-treasure hunt through cave sediment for fossils and tools, Changing Landscape – a study of past biological and geomorphological processes, Exploring Nature – a programme of ecological games for 7 to 13-year-olds, Discovery Trails – explore the countryside around Creswell Crags, Project Work – field study in archeology, ecology, geography, history, etc. for all ages.
Parties: School and coach parties are welcome but group bookings should be made well in advance by contacting the Visitor Centre. If writing please enclose a s.a.e.

Heights of Abraham

The Heights of Abraham are 35 acres (14 hectares) of landscaped woodland high on the southern slopes of Masson Hill, above the village of Matlock Bath. From a geological point of view they have a complex history. Millions of years ago mineral deposition changed much of the local limestone, which was sandwiched between two layers of volcanic rock, into dolomite. This in turn was partly dissolved away along fault lines to be replaced by mineral veins or 'rakes' of fluorspar, lead sulphide or galena, and barytes. The caves, left by underground streams which honeycombed the hill, became choked with debris carried down by the melting ice as glaciation receded at the end of the Great Ice Age. Masson Hill sits astride the Bacon or Great Rake, one of Derbyshire's most notable mineral veins, and it was caverns like Great Masson, filled with alluvial ore, that attracted the medieval miners or 'old men'.

Traditionally lead has been mined in the vicinity of Masson Hill since Roman times, but the first documented evidence of underground work, as opposed to surface mining, being carried out on the hill itself, is for Nestus, mentioned in a list of mines compiled in 1470. By the end of the eighteenth century hundreds of years of concentrated lead mining around the Nestus Mine had taken its toll, turning the southern slopes of Masson Hill into an industrial wasteland. And then, suddenly, it was all over. In 1780 part of the hill was enclosed to form an estate known as the Heights of Abraham – at the time it was thought to resemble the famous heights at Quebec, stormed by general Wolfe in 1759.

The bare slopes were extensively planted as a forest garden with picturesque zig-zag pathways and exotic flowered shrubberies. During this period, Matlock Bath had become a famous spar, encouraging the developers of the Heights to open the Great Rutland Show Cavern to the public in 1810. In 1844 Great Masson was also opened, the Victoria Prospect Tower was built and refreshments were provided from a rustic building on the site of the present Hillside Tavern, which boasts the oldest beer license in either Matlock or Matlock Bath.

By the late 1970s the once-magnificent landscaped gardens had become seriously delapidated and the first phase of restoration was put in hand. Footpaths were rebuilt, over-mature trees felled and the original shrub borders recovered from the enveloping undergrowth. The gardens were then replanted along the lines of the original 'savage' garden. The big break-through came in the spring of 1984 with the commissioning of the first alpine-style cable car system in Britain. The punishing climb to the top of the Heights had always been a problem. Now it became possible for young and old alike to journey to the top in comfort in all weathers, soaring gracefully over the Derwent Valley, the railway and the Derby road to the new Treetops Visitor Centre. With its superb

Continued overleaf

views over the woodland to the hills beyond the Derwent it is a splendid place to relax and talk, eat or drink amidst sylvan surroundings high above the busy town.

Until recently hurricane lamps and candles were all that was offered to light the visitor's way through the show caverns. Now both Great Masson and Nastus Mine are properly lit for the first time in their long history, revealing many exciting features that were not readily seen before. Underground, the visitor can explore the old workings and experience the atmosphere and sounds of a Derbyshire lead mine in action, seeing a variety of minerals such as calcite, malachite, barytes and fluorspar. Everything at the Heights of Abraham is supremely well presented and, after buying a ticket at the Base Station, the entire complex is at your disposal. There is no other place quite like it in Britain and few that even approach it in quality and standard of presentation.

General Information

Owner: Heights of Abraham (Matlock Bath) Ltd
Title: Great Masson Cavern and Great Rutland Cavern–Nestus Mine
Location: Heights of Abraham, Matlock Bath, Derbyshire.
Enquiries: The Manager, Heights of Abraham
Telephone: 0629 2365
Directions: The Centre of Matlock Bath on A6 north of Derby.
Access: Open daily Easter to October 10 a.m.–5 p.m.
Nearest car park: Ample free car/coach parking at Matlock Bath Station.
Distance: 220 yards (200 metres)
Time to explore: Two or three hours
Conditions: Dry graded footpaths throughout. There are a series of steps in Great Masson Cavern.
Facilities: Tree Tops Visitor Centre comprising restaurant, licensed bar, coffee shop, extensive gift shop. Picnic area; tavern and tea terrace; lavatories. Multivision Pavilion showing how the cavern was formed. Audio-visual show describing the history of lead mining. Cable car from Matlock Station to Tree Tops Centre. Victoria Tower.
Parties: School and coach parties welcome.

Odin Mine

Odin Mine is the oldest recorded lead mine in Derbyshire and is reputed to have been worked in Saxon and possibly even Roman times. In 1663 the workings had become so extensive that there was a dispute over ownership. It was worked continuously throughout the eighteenth century. The open cleft of the Odin Gorge lies to the left of the truncated A625 facing Mam Tor, a short distance past Treak Cliff Cavern. The gash in the hillside is in fact purely artificial, formed when the large out-cropping vein was completely removed. From deep inside the narrow opening can be heard the sepulchral drip, drop, of water echoing back from the depths. While it is possible for the expert to descend into the old workings at the rear of the gorge with the aid of ladders, this is not to be recommended as they are known to be highly dangerous, being close to the point of collapse in places.

On the opposite side of the road to the Odin Gorge lies the Knowles Shaft and the well-preserved remains of an old ore-crushing circle with its gritstone wheel and tyre. Evidence of the position of the main Rake Workings can be traced for a distance of about half a mile (0.8 kilometres) towards Mam Tor at the head of the valley. One of the old entrances, Tinker's Shaft, is buried under the road by the Blue John Cavern. The area is now in the care of the National Trust. Tranquil sheep now graze on the hillocks that were once heaps of mine spoil and, with the Hope Valley stretching away below into the distance, on a fine, clear day it is a decidedly pleasant area in which to picnic.

General Information

Owner: National Trust
Title: Odin Mine
Location: Western end of Hope Valley. Map reference OS sheet 119 134834
Enquiries: National Trust Regional Office, Clumber Park Stableyard, Worksop, Nottinghamshire
Telephone: 0909 486411

Directions: From Castleton follow the A625 to the north avoiding Winnats Pass. Follow the signs to Treak Cliff Cavern and continue to the end of the road. The footpath to the mine is marked by a National Trust sign.
Access: Any reasonable time
Nearest car park: Free car/coach parking on site

Distance: 110 yards (100 metres)
Time to explore: Half an hour
Conditions: Open dale site. Stout footwear is recommended. Always beware of unfenced shafts.
Facilities: None.

Peak Cavern

The approach to Peak Cavern must be one of the most memorable sights in Britain. From Castleton the path skirts a babbling stream, past picturesque cottages, and enters a monumental limestone gorge. Ferns, creepers and trees cling bravely to the sides of the cliffs that in places are as much as 250 feet (75 metres) high and the air is filled with dancing sunlight and bird-song. Glowering over the top of the gorge is an ancient castle. Built by William Peveril some twenty years after the Norman Conquest it is from this robust old building that the small town derives its name.

Just inside the vast, funnel-like entrance, which, remarkably, has yet to be properly investigated archeologically, is the site of the now disused cavern ropeworks. Shielded by the towering cheeks of the cliff, the huge cave mouth is the largest entrance of any cavern in Europe and forms a natural underground workshop. Here, incredibly, centuries ago, a small village grew up, housing the workers who developed a thriving cottage industry making ropes for the local lead mines. Protected as they were from the elements by their unusual surroundings, these troglodytic ropemakers were able to carry on their craft in comparative comfort for over 400 years. The celebrated Ben Johnson was of the opinion that the industry was run by a community of tinkers, led by a fearsome robber-king, one Cock Laurel; certainly in his day the area was, apparently, carefully avoided by the locals. Rope continued to be spun here until 1974, when the last of the ropemakers, a Mr. Burt Morrison, retired at the venerable age of eighty-nine. His small iron machine or 'runner' is still to be seen, together with other primitive items of equipment with which he used to ply his trade.

The hazy blue light from the entrance penetrates deep into the heart of the cave, forming a somewhat eerie backdrop as it reflects off the convoluted sides and roof which are punctuated by formations of small stalactites. By the time the section known as Lumbago Walk has been reached, available daylight is virtually non-existent. Until fairly recently only the intrepid ventured past this point because it was necessary to embark on a short trip in a very small boat propelled under a very low arch by the guide. Many famous people were carried in this way including Queen Victoria; it is not recorded if the lugubrious Johnson ever succumbed to this indignity. Nowadays the terrors of the ferry-boat have been dispelled by the enlargement of the orifice.

The object of their curiosity was the next chamber which is over 150 feet (45 metres) wide, 90 feet (27 metres) long and 60 feet (18 metres) high, an enormous space considering it was hollowed out entirely by the action of water. Beyond the Great Cave a high passage leads to a perpetual cascade of water in Roger Rain's House. It was in this area that at one time visitors were entertained by choirs serenading them from a natural balcony high above the cave floor. This is the end of the tour for the general public, but experienced cavers can continue into the muddy crawls and tight rocky passages of the Far Reaches.

General Information

Owner: Duchy of Lancaster
Title: Peak Cavern
Location: Peak Cavern, Castleton, Sheffield, Derbyshire
Enquiries: The Custodian, Peak Cavern
Telephone: 0433 20285

Continued overleaf

Directions: The cavern is situated in the centre of Castleton beneath Peveril Castle.
Access: Open daily, Easter to October, 10 a.m.–5 p.m. Closed on Mondays in winter.
Nearest car park: Free car/coach parking on site
Distance: 330 yards (300 metres)
Time to explore: 45 minutes

Conditions: Mainly dry graded footpaths throughout. There are several flights of shallow steps which can, with a little difficulty, be negotiated by wheelchair.
Facilities: Covered waiting area. Small souvenir shop selling confectionery, hot and cold drinks. Potholing by arrangement.
Parties: School and coach parties welcome.

Poole's Cavern

Poole's Cavern has been a successful show cave since 1853 and was a popular venue in Victorian times. Prior to this the cave was wide open and could be entered by the inquisitive, provided they were prepared to crawl the first 65 feet (20 metres) or so on their hands and knees equipped with a length of tallow candle or a wooden torch. During this 'unofficial' part of its history, Poole's Cavern became very well known indeed, people coming from far and wide to view the secrets contained therein. Unfortunately, vandalism and souvenir hunting caused considerable damage to the stalactite formations. The Duke of Devonshire, who owned the cavern at the time, became concerned and invited Frank Redfern, a local man, to try to run the caves for the benefit of tourists. He dug out the entrance and illuminated the caverns with candles until, in 1859, gas lights were installed. It was still illuminated by this method until the last of the Redfern family owners died.

In 1975 the Duke of Devonshire donated the nearby Grin Low Wood to Buxton and District Civic Association who immediately purchased Poole's Cavern, making the cave and wood into the Buxton Country Park. Poole's cavern is an entirely natural cave and despite earlier disfigurement still has some of the finest formations to be seen in the British Isles. To many visitors it is a source of wonder that such marvels of nature are wrought entirely by the action of water either rushing through cavities in the rock to create the vast halls, or dripping for countless centuries through faults in the roof and walls. Indeed, the view down the 330 yard (300 metre) length of the cave from the balcony towards the bridge over the Derbyshire River Wye, which flows through part of the cave, has been described as one of the finest underground views in the country. The vista takes in many features of the cave, including the Roman Chamber, a huge stalactite known as the Flitch of Bacon and multiple gour pools. The highlight of the tour is considered by many to be the so-called Poached Egg Chamber. Here almost every possible type of cave formation can be observed from stalactites and stalagmites, straws and columns to flowstone cascades and curtains.

There is a strong possibility that the site once contained the only known one-man Romano-British bronze jewellery workshop in the British Isles. In 1981 the Peak District Archeological Society under the direction of Dr Donald Bramwell carried out a dig near Royal Chamber, some 33 yards (30 metres) inside the cave, where they were rewarded by finding over a dozen items of Roman bronze jewellery. The dig continued for three years and during this time over 4,000 items were found including the bones of animals that had been consumed as food, pottery, including fragments of Roman Samian ware, Roman coins and a few items of iron and leather. The pick of the items found are currently on display in the Visitor Centre along with a history of man's use of the cave over the past 5,000 years.

General Information

Owner: The Buxton and District Civic Association Ltd
Title: Poole's Cavern Buxton Country Park
Location: Buxton Country Park, Grin Low Woods, Poole's Cavern, Green Lane, Buxton, Derbyshire
Enquiries: Poole's Cavern
Telephone: 0298 6978
Directions: From the centre of Buxton take St John's Road and turn left into Burlington Road. Cross into Temple Road, turn left into Green Lane and follow the signs for Poole's Cavern.

Continued on page 97

Guide Peter Arfield leads the way through the
comparative comfort of Bagshawe's 'Trip One' section
– there is a Trip Three, but that is only for the
masochistic (page 79)

Left
An elderly shovel marks the veins of the rare Blue John stone embedded in semi-transparent fluorspar (page 80)

Opposite
Modern cable cars link Matlock Bath Station with the superb new Heights of Abraham visitor centre at Derbyshire's oldest tourist attraction (page 85)

Below
There are a total of twenty-five known caves hidden in the woods which screen Creswell Crags, one of the world's key archeological heritage sites (page 84)

This artificial gorge is the only surviving entrance to
the dangerous complex of disused shafts and unstable
stopes of Odin, the oldest recorded mine in Derbyshire
(page 86)

Opposite
The amazing cave entrance at Peak Cavern which not
all that long ago housed a small village with its
attendant rope-making works. The local name for the
cleft is 'The Devil's Hole' (page 87)

Opposite
Poole's Cavern is an impressive natural cave which not only boasts Roman connections but some very unusual straw stalactite formations (page 88)

Right
A wall of 'deads' and a mine tub used for tramming fluorite to the surface in the Peak District Mines Historical Society's Temple Mine (page 98)

Below
Like a cluster of exotic worms these colourful stalactites hang from the roof of Treak Cliff Cavern, famous for its deposits of the valuable and highly decorative Blue John (page 99)

Right
Carved out of the
sandstone of Castle
Rock, the Rock Lounge
of Nottingham's historic
Trip to Jerusalem Inn
could no doubt tell some
tales if only we had the
means of listening
(page 100)

Below
The eccentric fifth Duke
of Portland's under-
ground stables at Welbeck
Abbey (page 101)

Access: Open daily, Easter to October 10 a.m.–5 p.m. Closed Wednesdays during April, May and October.
Nearest car park: Ample free car/coach park nearby
Distance: 55 yards (50 metres)
Time to explore: 45 minutes
Conditions: Smooth, graded mainly level pathways. There are three short flights of steps easily negotiated by wheelchair.

Facilities: Cavern gift shop selling confectionery, ices, soft drinks, souvenirs and books; lavatories including facilities for handicapped persons. A limited number of wheelchairs available on request. Visitor Centre exhibition with video. An Education Pack is available for schools. The Buxton and District Civic Association Ltd is a charitable organization.
Parties: School and coach parties welcome.

Speedwell Cavern

Situated beside the old coaching road at the foot of Winnats Pass, Speedwell Cavern is a disused lead mine. Mining started there in 1771, when an attempt was made to intersect the main lead veins of Longcliff Rake. Unfortunately Faucet Rake, the primary objective, was found to have been washed out. The level was extended further but, after tunnelling for a total of some half mile (0.8 kilometres) through solid limestone, a series of underground streams were encountered near New Rake. Undeterred, the ingenious miners elected to flood the tunnel, thereby forming a miniature canal enabling boats to be used for the laborious business of transporting waste rock and ore. Despite their resourcefulness, the adventurers' efforts were not rewarded with the quality of ore for which they hoped and mining was discontinued about 1790.

The miners used to have to climb down a vertical shaft to reach their place of work but the modern tourist has the luxury of a flight of steps. The steep, dry-stone, arched passage penetrates into the depths of the hillside and gives access to a small jetty suspended on chains over the head of what must surely be the most unique underground waterway in Britain. From this rudimentary landing stage battery-powered punts depart every fifteen minutes on a voyage worthy of a story by Jules Verne. With barely sufficient headroom to sit upright one is propelled in eerie silence the length of the echoing, starlit tunnel, to the awesome cavern known as the Bottomless Pit, an underground chasm as tall as a church spire. Formed by the erosion of part of Faucet Rake, it is said that this spectacular pot hole swallowed some 40,000 tons of rubble without any effect on the

water level. After heavy rain, water pours down this abyss to disappear for a period of twenty-two hours before emerging only half a mile away at a spring called Russet Well in the village of Castleton. On the wall an illuminated plan gives some idea of the extensive cave systems which beckon the intrepid beyond the strong, iron railings guarding the brink of the yawning gulf. There are literally miles of confined crouch-ways, crawls and syphons, punctuated with caverns; death-traps for any but the experienced potholer.

With the winking double lights of the tunnel leading back to the steep stone steps and daylight on the one hand and Far Canal, a further flooded level, disappearing into the darkness towards the old flooded workings on the other, it is worth standing for a moment and sparing a thought for the eighteenth-century miners who worked there. Scraping a living from the unyielding Peak limestone with little more than hand tools must have been no sinecure. Mining was abandoned at the turn of the century, only to be resumed once more for a few years before finally ending in 1814, by which time visitors were already being taken below ground to see the sights. It seems sad that, after all their efforts, 't'owd men' could not make the undertaking pay.

General Information

Owners: R J and Mrs J H and K Harrison
Title: Speedwell Cavern
Location: Winnats Pass, Castleton, Derbyshire
Enquiries: Speedwell Cavern Ltd
Telephone: 0433 20512
Directions: Take the A625 to the west of Castleton and after half a mile (0.8 kilometres) turn left into Winnats Pass.

Continued overleaf

Access: Open daily throughout the year, 9.30 a.m.–5.30 p.m.
Nearest car park: Free car/coach park opposite the entrance.
Distance: 22 yards (20 metres)
Time to explore: 45 minutes
Conditions: A flight of steps gives access to an underground canal along which visitors travel by boat. The caves are unsuitable for those not able-bodied.

Facilities: There is a gift shop at the entrance which specializes in a fine selection of jewellery and ornaments made in Blue John stone. Confectionery, soft drinks and light refreshments are available from the kiosk. Lavatories.
Parties: School parties welcome at reduced rates by arrangement.

Temple Mine

Temple Mine was opened in 1922 for the extraction of fluorite, a mineral commonly used as a smelting flux in the iron and steel industry. Abandoned only three years later as unprofitable, it was re-opened and extended in the 1950s, operating on a strict policy of only working the richest ground. This time it proved more successful and headings were developed on two levels. Originally linked by a steep incline this has now been replaced by a flight of steps. During the last few years of working an ore hopper and shoot system were installed to drop ore to the lower level. Walls on either side of the hopper were built of waste rock. Constructions using 'deads' are commonly encountered underground. Building retaining walls, supporting roofs or even back-filling dangerous areas, apart from serving a useful purpose, also meant that less spoil had to be carted to surface – a big consideration in a mine. The Peak District Mines Historical Society took over ownership in 1975 by the ancient Derbyshire custom of 'nicking'.

The mine can be visited on its own, but since it effectively forms a field study for the extremely interesting Peak District Mining Museum at the Pavilion in the centre of Matlock Bath, it is well worth combining the two. Lead mining is one of Derbyshire's oldest industries, its history stretching back over 2,000 years. The Peak District Mining Museum displays are designed to show the work of the lead miner through the ages. If you want not only to find out what kibbles and wiskets, sloughs and coffin levels, stemples and stowes are, but would quite like to see examples on display, this is the place. Sensibly set out in chronological order, the exhibits trace the pattern of progress as it affected the miner at the face, as simple hand tools were superceded by increasingly sophisticated equipment and methods.

The huge water-pressure engine on display is a case in point. Dating back to 1819 and the drawing board of no lesser man than the celebrated Cornish engineer Richard Trevithick, it was found virtually intact in a 394 feet (120 metre) deep shaft at Wills Founder Mine near Winster. Driven by a 164 feet (50 metre) head of water operating a piston, this massive piece of ironwork de-watered a level 98 feet (30 metres) below itself at the rate of 200 gallons (910 litres) per minute. Although that may not seem much now, at the beginning of the nineteenth century it represented a tremendous step forward in mining technology, not to mention a useful saving in coal-steam equivalent.

For those with time to linger a while, there is much to find of interest, such as an enormous Roman ingot of lead found near Ashbourne. There are sections on rocks and minerals, prospecting, excavation and stoping, underground transport, drainage and mining law, the strange and ancient rights and customs enjoyed by the old lead-mining men. For more agile people the museum has thoughtfully built a maze of twisted tunnels to crawl through, specially reconstructed so that the visitor can, in perfect safety, experience for themselves something of the cramped, claustrophobic conditions which were the lot of a Peak District lead miner in the last century.

General Information
Owner: The Peak District Mines Historical Society Ltd
Title: Temple Mine
Location: Temple Walk, Matlock Bath, Derbyshire
Enquiries: The Manager Peak District Mining Museum, The Pavilion, Matlock Bath, Derbyshire

Telephone: 0629 3834
Directions: From the centre of Matlock Bath take the A6 towards Derby. After passing the Pavilion Mining Museum on the left turn first right and follow the signs. On foot take the footpath opposite the museum alongside the 'Fishpond' and follow the signs for Temple Mine.
Access: Mine: open daily, Easter to October 11 a.m.–4 p.m. Weekdays in summer season 10 a.m.–5 p.m. November to March, weekends only, 2 p.m.–4 p.m. Museum: open daily mid-February to mid-November and weekends throughout the year 11 a.m.–4 p.m.
Nearest car park: Local Authority car parks off Temple Walk and beside the Pavilion Mining Museum.
Distance: 110 yards (100 metres) from Temple Walk car park, 330 yards (300 metres) from the Pavilion Museum

Time to explore: Allow half an hour
Conditions: Graded footpaths throughout with original mine-tub railway track still in *situ*. There is a short flight of steps and the roof is low in places. Stout footwear is recommended. Protective headgear is provided free.
Facilities: Small gift shop at mine entrance selling confectionery. Well stocked shop selling gifts, souvenirs and books on a range of general and specialist subjects at the Pavilion Mining Museum. There is an impressive collection of lead mining artefacts on display at the Pavilion Museum. Exhibits include an original 1819 Trevithick water-pressure engine. The museum bookshop also provides one of the best selections of books on hard-rock mining in Britain.
Parties: School parties and coach parties welcome. Group tours for school parties provided by arrangement.

Treak Cliff Cavern

The village of Castleton, in the heart of the Peak District in Derbyshire, is famous world-wide for its caves, its castle and its Blue John. An extremely rare variety of fluorspar, Blue John is peculiar to Treak Cliff hill. Quite when it was first discovered is a mystery, but it is recorded that by the year 1770 some sixteen mines were working the area, supplying something like thirty small workshops in Castleton, Buxton and Matlock, with this exquisite dark-blue or purple-veined mineral. Here craftsmen fashioned it into goblets, urns, vases and even fireplaces for stately homes. HM the Queen has a particularly fine collection of articles made from this material which in essence is nothing more nor less than an exotic form of dis-coloured crystalline calcium fluoride.

The Treak Cliff reaches a height of about 1300 feet (400 metres) although it is not strictly cliff at all but a steep-sided hill that looms at the western end of the Hope Valley to the left of the now-closed road to Mam Tor. The entrance to the cavern is at the top of a stepped footpath winding steeply above the road. Treak Cliff caves themselves were hollowed out by underground rivers many thousands of years ago and are divided into two main sections. The first part was discovered by lead miners looking for likely lodes in 1750. The second range was opened up by prospectors searching for new veins of Blue John in 1926. Both of these sections were opened to members of the public in 1935. Mining for the mineral, however, still

continues over the winter months.

During the guided tour, which takes in both the old and new sections, visitors are shown the largest piece of Blue John ever discovered. Taking the form of a massive pillar some 6 feet (1.8 metres) thick and 16 tons (16.26 tonnes) in weight, it supports the roof of one of the Witches' Caves and must surely be the most valuable prop in Derbyshire. Besides veins of Blue John there are many other interesting features to be seen. Further into the hill, towards the end of the second part of the system, in an untouched section of the cave, there is a beautiful, natural formation consisting of literally hundreds of particularly colourful, well-formed stalactites and stalagmites. J. W. Puttrell, the great speleologist and caver, suggested that the area should be named 'The Dream Cave' as it epitomizes what cavers dream about but rarely find.

General Information

Owner: Harold Harrison
Title: Treak Cliff Cavern
Location: Castleton, Sheffield
Enquiries: Treak Cliff Cavern
Telephone: 0433 20571
Directions: From Castleton follow the A625 to the north avoiding Winnats Pass and the cavern is signposted.
Access: Open daily 9.30 a.m.–6 p.m. in summer and 9.30 a.m.–4.30 p.m. in winter. Closed Christmas Day.
Nearest car park: Free car/coach parking on site
Distance: 165 yards (150 metres)
Time to explore: 45 minutes

Continued overleaf

Conditions: Dry, smooth footpaths. There are numerous flights of steps. The roof is low in places. The cavern is unsuitable for the disabled, the visually handicapped or those suffering from circulatory or respiratory conditions.

Facilities: Hot and cold snacks, confectionery and ice cream; gift shop selling a wide range of souvenirs; picnic area; lavatories; dogs allowed on leads.
Parties: School and coach parties welcome.

Trip to Jerusalem

The name of the Inn commemorates the third crusade and it is thought highly likely that men-at-arms who answered the call of Richard Ceur de Lion, in 1189, to crusade against the Saracens, called here as a welcome rest before marching to the Channel ports for embarkation. Nottingham Castle was a royal stronghold much favoured by the King, Richard I – as anyone acquainted with the minstrel's tales of the fair Maid Marian and Robin Hood of Sherwood Forest will no doubt tell you. The castle would therefore have been the local recruitment centre and it does not take much imagination to picture the merry-making that must have taken place hereabouts on such occasions.

The Trip to Jerusalem nestles against the foot of a vast lump of sandstone which goes under the somewhat unoriginal local name of Castle Rock. Crowned by the castle, the rock is honeycombed with a complex maze of caves and underground passages which lead right under and into the castle itself. The Trip is so steeped in history the visitor gets the impression that the very walls of the small cavern-like rooms are a veritable mine of mystery and intrigue. Notable amongst these is Mortimer's room which has a particularly gruesome story attached to it. Legend has it that the scatologically inclined Roger Mortimer, paramour of Queen Isabella the wife of King Edward II whom he so horribly murdered, used to meet his mistress in secret, presumably to mutter sweet plots in her shell-like ears. A small passageway links up with the aforementioned maze and it is thought that it was down this quaint facility that the good lady tip-toed. It is an unlikely tale as they could have had the castle virtually to themselves, but it adds a little spice. Roger came to a suitably sticky end at Tyburn after a dawn raid led by a somewhat upset Edward III who found him, low and behold, in the castle's royal apartments!

Another intriguing cave-room is reached by a stair from the central bar. Known as the Rock Lounge, it features a massive chimney that extends more than 60 feet (18 metres) through solid rock. It was once the malting room of the nearby Old Brewhouse. Festooned with objects which range from a Cromwellian helmet to a collection of interesting old clocks, it is rumoured that further passages exist connecting the Rock Lounge with another system of underground passages beneath the castle. The Back Room, which is pure seventeenth century and, as one would expect, at the back of the premises, and the Ward Room both have interesting histories which are described in a handy booklet which can be purchased from the bar.

The cellars of the Trip are fascinating. Extending from near the entrance of the inn itself they continue on a slight declivity some 33 yards (30 metres) beyond the curtilage to a point beneath Castle Rock almost directly below the bandstand which is in the castle grounds. At the end of the tunnel there is an ancient cock-fighting pit dating back to the times when the bygone equivalent of today's lager-louts drank beer and partook in a spot of gambling deep underground. Appropriately enough, nearby there are two smaller caves, one a plain dungeon, the other reserved for those condemned to die on the local gallows.

For centuries real beer was brewed for the inn in the Brewhouse, a cave situated directly beneath the Rock Lounge. Initially the beer or porter was produced exclusively for the castle, supplies to the inn only being forthcoming later and continuing until about forty years ago when supply could not keep pace with demand. Nowadays the visitor will find a wide selection of real ales for his or her delectation.

The historic Brewhouse Yard can be found at the foot of Castle Rock, only a few seconds walk from the notable public house the Trip to Jerusalem Inn. The museum has been established on the site of the Old Brewhouse caves. To the west can be seen the railed off entrances to a passage which leads into the network of caves which honeycomb the castle rock.

Other interesting caves open to the public in Nottingham are the Bridlesmithgate Caves at Bridlesmithgate which are the subject of a guided tour lasting approximately one hour. Further information can be obtained from the Tours Organizer of the Nottingham Historical and Archeological Society by telephoning 0602 785503 or from the Curator of the Brewhouse Yard Museum, telephone 0602 483504.

General Information

Owner: Mr E Marshall
Title: Trip to Jerusalem Inn
Location: Castle Road, Nottingham
Enquiries: The Manager
Telephone: 0602 473171
Directions: At the foot of Castle Rock
Access: Normal public house opening times.
Nearest car park: Limited car parking on Castle Road. National Car Park at Collin Street.
Distance: 440 yards (400 metres)
Time to explore: Half an hour
Conditions: Dry convivial atmosphere
Facilities: Licensed bars; hot and cold snacks; lavatories
Parties: By arrangement with the management.

Welbeck Abbey

Welbeck Abbey today is run as a residential college. Founded in 1953 it provides suitable candidates with a sixth-form education designed to equip them for professional service in the army's technical corps. But this modern role tends to disguise the fact that the abbey itself has had a remarkably chequered history prior to becoming a gateway to a commission in the army. The original Premonstratensian Abbey was founded almost exactly 700 years before the present college and enjoyed three relatively unexceptional centuries until the establishment was dissolved by Henry VIII and passed into the hands of one Richard Whalley. From then on the place changed hands many times, coming under the influence of the formidable Bess of Hardwick, who purloined it for her son, Sir Charles Cavendish. During the Civil War it was lost to the Roundheads, only to be recaptured, belonged briefly to the Earl of Clare, then the richest man in England, was passed on to the Countess of Oxford whose daughter married the second Duke of Portland, in whose family it has remained ever since.

Naturally changes were made as succeeding owners exercised their particular fancies or eccentricities, but none made changes so far reaching nor so eccentric as the decidedly potty fifth Duke whose lot it was to take over the estate in 1860. Anyone inheriting a historic abbey surrounded by 3,000 acres of Sherwood Forest landscaped by Repton, could be excused for indulging their whim a little perhaps, but to create one of the largest ball rooms in the world, a roller-skating rink, a kitchen so far from the dining hall that rails had to be laid to transport the food, stables, coach houses and a garden – all underground – and then to spend his life living in three rooms, was surely pushing the limits of reason just a bit. Perhaps it would not have looked quite so bad if he had entertained right royally, but he did not. He was shy and retiring and disliked society so much that he spent a large small fortune having tunnels excavated under the gardens so that he could move around his estate, or indeed leave it if the mood so took him, unseen by anyone but his coachman and valet.

And yet perhaps he was not all that mad after all, except about horses; his pride and joy was his riding school, the second largest in Europe. After completing that in 1869, his next major venture was the construction of the underground ballroom, begun in 1875. The Duke intended it to be a chapel. Some chapel! It measures 159 feet by 63 feet (48 metres by 19

Continued overleaf

metres) and remains one of the largest private rooms built without supporting pillars in the world. But it is the extraordinary series of tunnels that make the enigmatical mind of the man who planned them seem so intriguing. There are literally miles of them; the longest runs underground from the house, dives under the lake and emerges over a mile away at the old Worksop road. The question arises, could there have been some ulterior motive for his wanting to go and come as he pleased? We shall never know; he died in London in 1879 without offering a satisfactory reason for his little eccentricity. Maybe he was not that daft after all.

One thing is certain, his underground extravagances are very eerie, empty places to visit now. Underground stables and coach houses are deserted and forlorn, the ground-level glazed roof over the stable yard is overgrown with brambles, the iron frames are rusting and forgotten. There are suites of small, functional rooms, some of which were obviously once expensively appointed. Did the fifth Duke await his carriage here? And then there are the tunnels themselves, high enough and wide enough for two mail coaches to pass, brick-lined and dry as a stick, and about as secretive. And so the question remains, why did the Duke build these tunnels? What could have possessed him to want to move from his suite of rooms in the abbey to the world beyond his extensive estate with as few people as possible seeing his face? Soldiers don't ask questions.

General Information

Owner: Duke and Duchess of Portland
Title: Welbeck Abbey Underground Tunnels
Location: Welbeck College, Worksop, Nottinghamshire
Enquiries: The Bursar, Welbeck College
Access: Welbeck College is an MOD Army Residential College. It is NOT open to the public.

THE NORTH

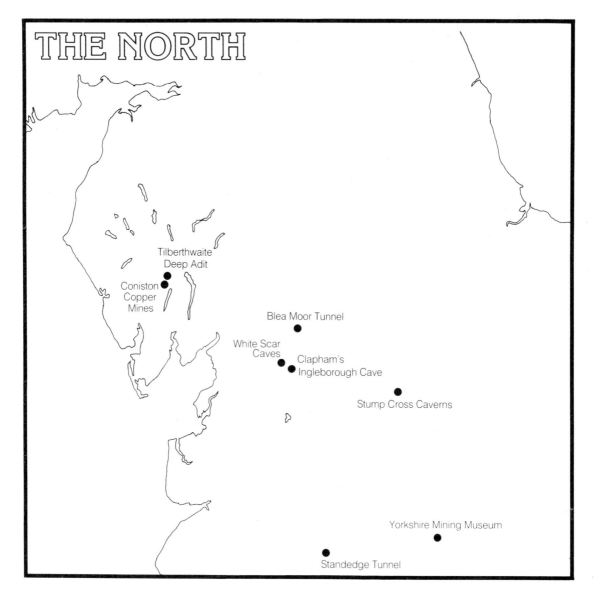

Tilberthwaite
Deep Adit

Coniston
Copper
Mines

Blea Moor Tunnel

White Scar
Caves

Clapham's
Ingleborough Cave

Stump Cross Caverns

Yorkshire Mining Museum

Standedge Tunnel

The Pennine chain offered a tremendous challenge to engineers and locomotive men alike during the pioneer years of the railways. The two tunnels included in this section, Blea Moor, on the picturesque Settle–Carlisle line and Standedge on what was the old London and South Western line linking Manchester to Huddersfield, effectively determine the northern and southern boundaries of our northern region. Both are typical in their way and indicative of the great railway drive of the nineteenth century which took the permanent way over and through the Pennines, the very

backbone of England. There are of course others, such as the Midland Railway's 3 miles 950 yards (5,700 metres) tunnel west of Totely, the longest British tunnel after the 4 miles 628 yards (7 kilometres) Severn Tunnel, on a line that also passed through the lengthy Cowburn Tunnel on its way from Chapel-en-le-Frith to Sheffield. The multiple tunnels of Standedge, at 3 miles 90 yards (4,900 metres) are the next longest and are particularly interesting as they run parallel with the Huddersfield Narrow Canal. The Sheffield, Ashton and Manchester Railway's Woodhead Tunnel, at just over 3

Continued overleaf

miles (4,835 metres), when it was completed in 1845 was the longest tunnel on any railway in the country. It also had the reputation of being arguably the foulest tunnel in the world, with the possible exception of the infamous first section of the London Metropolitan.

The Pennines of course are a caver's paradise, being literally honeycombed with natural caves and pot holes most of which are only accessible to experienced potholers. Stump Cross, White Scar and Ingleborough are, however, accessible and well worth visiting.

Over to the west of the region, much as Blaenafon's Big Pit puts Welsh deep seam mining into perspective, so Caphouse Colliery and Mining Museum near Wakefield gives members of the public an opportunity to see the realities of working down one of the oldest coal mines in Yorkshire. Like its counterpart in Wales, this is no sinecure, this is the real thing. Ex-miners acting as guides kit the visitor up with helmets and miners' lamps and show him how coal has been mined down the ages. If you want to learn all about 'black gold' this is the place to go. On the other hand, if guided tours are not your cup of tea and you feel up to a little gentle exploration on your own, there is no better place to start than the copper mining area of Coniston, in the heart of Wordsworth's unique, inimitable Lake District, where sun, mist, cloud, water and mountain provide an ever-changing panorama that at times can be visually as well as physically breathtaking.

Blea Moor Tunnel

The extraordinarily spectacular Settle to Carlisle line stands monument to British mountain railway building in general and the engineering self-confidence of the Midland Railway in particular. While, by completing the line through Matlock and the Peak District, the company gained a means of access to Manchester, the ultimate aim was to build a railway through the Pennines and thereby reach the Scottish border at Carlisle. When the line was opened in 1876 linking Leeds and West Yorkshire with Carlisle and Glasgow, it became the third route from England to Scotland, the other two being the York–Newcastle–Edinburgh to the east and the Crewe–Carlisle–Glasgow to the west. While not belittling the achievements of either of the other two, from the point of view of ease of construction, their problems, Shap Fell notwithstanding, were child's play in comparison to the difficulties encountered, and overcome, by the engineers of the good old Midland.

Set amidst the idyllic scenery of the North Yorkshire Moors, Blea Moor Tunnel is an integral part of that famous line, built in the best spirit of British railway engineering. The Long Drag, as the line was known, is some 71 miles (115 kilometres) in length and runs up and over the Pennines reaching a summit of 1,100 feet (335 metres) making it the highest main line in England. Blea Moor Tunnel and the magnificent Ribblehead Viaduct which is nearby are very much a part of the history of our national railways. Stone for the Riblehead Viaduct, with its twenty-four arches rising 100 feet (33 metres) was quarried in the tunnel with pick and shovel and transported by horse and wheelbarrow, frequently in appalling weather. The viaduct stands as a testimony to the skill and fortitude of the Victorian engineer and navigator. During the tunnel's construction, 2,000 navvies slaved on the project and there were 200 deaths; one in ten! The traverse between Blea Moor and Dent Head was considered miraculous at the time and today forms part of what many consider to be 'England's Greatest Scenic Railway'. Ten stations remain operational, and there are a number, in addition, which are now closed but still boast the maroon and white lettered name boards of the Midland Railway. Much of the fine, cast iron tracery of the roof canopies is also still extant and hopefully one day these stations will be restored to play the role for which they were

Continued on page 109

Obscured by the steam belching from *Mallard*, Blea Moor Tunnel on the Settle–Carlisle line stands as a permanent monument to British mountain railway building (page 104)

Rusting and forgotten, a soul surviving belt-wheel casts Victorian shadows over the ruins of the Bonsor dressing floors at Coniston Copperworks (page 110)

Right
Fed by the waters of Fell Beck, the
364 feet (111 metre) depth of
Gaping Gill's Main Shaft was first
descended by the celebrated
French caver, Eduard Martell
in 1895 (page 109)
(David Crutchey)

Below
Tilberthwaite Horse Crag Level
deep adit which leads to the
slate cavern or 'closehead'
excavated by John 'Willie'
Shaw (page 113)

The impressive amber-coloured curtain in the recently
opened Wolverine Cave at Stump Cross Caverns
(page 112)

Scoured out of the Great Scar limestone by thousands of years of aqueous erosion, White Scar Caves still has its own stream running beneath the board-walk (page 115)

At Caphouse Colliery ex-miners are on hand to guide visitors through the difficult and potentially dangerous world of the coal-face worker in a mine that only ceased production in 1985 (page 116)

originally designed and built.

On a sunny day from Blea Moor it is possible to see for miles but local weather is particularly treacherous and in only a quarter of an hour can change completely. One year, on 1st June at 6.30 a.m. over 3 inches (7.6 centimetres) of snow fell near Blea Moor tunnel. By 10.30 a.m. it had completely gone and the sun was shining. In good weather, however, for those who enjoy rough walking and getting away from the encroachment of daily life, the scenery it is difficult to beat. In places the moor gives the impression of being almost a primeval natural wilderness so beset is it with rocks and mire through which wise walkers tread warily. All that can be heard are the sounds of moorland birds and stealthy growth of nature.

Of course one could spend all day there and never stand the remotest chance of seeing the *Mallard*; to catch even a glimpse of the world's fastest steam locomotive in action is very much a question of being at the right place at the right time. We just happened to be lucky. For the uninitiated, *Mallard* is the most celebrated of the London and North Eastern Railway Class A4 Pacifics. Designed by Sir Nigel Gresley to haul the crack 'Coronation' expresses of the 1930s, these cunningly streamlined locomotives regularly covered the 393 miles (630 kilo-metres) between King's Cross and Edinburgh in six hours non-stop. Just to prove their point, on 3rd July 1938, encouraged by official LNER instructions to 'give her all she'd got' over a section of line between Stoke and Peterborough, *Mallard* was coaxed up to the remarkable speed of 128 miles per hour (205 kilometres per hour). This still stands as the highest officially recorded speed of any steam locomotive. Of course the Settle to Carlisle line is far from her old haunts, but if the line could be opened as a private railway, who knows what excitements might be in store for steam enthusiasts?

General Information

Owner: British Rail
Title: Blea Moor Tunnel
Location: Blea Moor, Yorkshire Dales National Park, Yorkshire. Map reference OS sheet 98 775838
Enquiries: Settle Station
Telephone: 07292 3536
Directions: From Ingleton take the B6255 following the sign to Hawes. About 4 miles (6.4 kilometres) after the junction with the B6479 turn left onto a minor road signposted Stone House and Dent. The road crosses the railway line. The tunnel mouth is approximately 875 yards (800 metres) to the left of the bridge.
Access: Any reasonable time
Nearest car park: Adjoining minor road
Distance: 440 yards (400 metres)
Time to explore: Half an hour.
Conditions: Moorland tunnel. Please do not trespass on British Rail property.
Facilities: None.

Clapham's Ingleborough Cave

To get to Clapham's Ingleborough Cave there is no alternative but to walk, and an extremely pleasant walk it is too – in fine weather. The cave is to be found something over one mile (1.6 kilometres) north-east of the village of Clapham. It is best to leave vehicles in the well-signposted car park at the National Parks Centre and prepare for a steepish walk past church and waterfall through the grounds of a country estate. To find the way all one needs to do is to follow the beck up upstream until the sawmill, powered incidentally by an economical water turbine, is reached. Do not be deterred by the likely stacks of lumber, the mill is still in use. Instead, boldly enter the yard and obtain a Grounds Ticket from the adjacent cottage. From then on it is child's play – always provided your child does not mind a prolonged healthy but gentle climb through Clapdale and the grounds of the Ingleborough Estate. The walk leads on past a fine lake, beside which the celebrated botanist Reginald Farrar localized over 100 new plant species from the Far East at the turn of the century, and takes the visitor on to the cave entrance. It is a good idea to allow plenty of time for this part of the journey and pause to admire the fine woods and scenery.

Ingleborough Cave is particularly impressive. The entrance is sheltered under a low natural arch, useful shelter in wet weather. The

Continued overleaf

salient features of the cave are quite striking, both as regards their quality and quantity, the colours of the formations being particularly fine. Access to the 'old cave' was limited to something of the order of 22 yards (20 metres) inside the hill, the way ahead being blocked by a substantial calcite barrier behind which was a large quantity of pent-up water. But, in 1837, the owner of the Ingleborough Estate had the barrier partly removed, allowing the water to escape and, when the level had subsided, revealing the further section which can be visited today. Yet more natural barriers were 'eased' in the ensuing period making the available cave system really seem quite extensive, in spite of the fact that it only stretches for 440 yards (400 metres), albeit a very absorbing 440 yards. The formations are extremely fine and this, combined with the evocative trickling and gurgling of underground streams, helps make the visit memorable and the hike to get there well worthwhile.

Much has been written about the cave at Ingleborough and its possible connection with other pot hole systems in the area. Beyond the farthest point on the tourist route, lies a further 2 miles (3.5 kilometres) of soggy passages, through which cavers of necessity are forced to crawl, in places with only a tiny air space between water and roof. For years there were protracted disputes on the subject of whether it was a possibility that there was a link between Ingleborough and the giant pot Gaping Gill. To set any worried minds at rest it has now been quite definitely confirmed that there is.

The mystery was solved on 28th May 1982 when, after a trip demanding courage, endurance and technical expertise of an extraordinary nature, a thirteen-man team proved the physical connection with Ingleborough Cave by descending Gaping Gill and emerging many hours later to the blinding lights of a television reception committee.

General Information

Owner: The Farrar Estate
Title: Clapham's Ingleborough Cave
Location: Clapham, North Yorkshire, via Lancaster. Map reference OS sheet 98 754711
Enquiries: The Manager, Clapham's Ingleborough Cave
Telephone: 04685 242
Directions: Clapham village is on the A65 Leeds to Kendal road 6 miles (10 kilometres) north-west of Giggleswick. From the National Park Information Centre follow the Clapham Beck upstream past the church. Obtain your Grounds Ticket from the cottage beside the sawmill and follow the path through the Ingleborough Estate Grounds to the open moorland and the cave entrance.
Access: Open daily, March to October 10.30 a.m.–5.30 p.m. At weekends and by appointment for the remainder of the year.
Nearest car park: Ample car/coach parking at Clapham National Parks Centre.
Distance: One mile (1.6 kilometres)
Time to explore: Guided tour 50 minutes. Allow at least one hour for the walk up to the cave and back.
Conditions: Good country pathways. Dry graded footpaths throughout the cave easily negotiated by wheelchair. Sensible footwear is rcommended.
Facilities: Confectionery, soft-drinks and light refereshments are avilable from the kiosk. Covered waiting area. There are cafés, gift shops and lavatories in Clapham village. An audio-visual presentation is planned.
Parties: Group tours for school and coach parties provided by arrangement.

Coniston Copper Mines

Since medieval times men have searched for wealth hidden deep within the fells. Coniston Copper Mines Valley was no exception and by 1885 over 500 people were at work above and below ground in what was to become for a time 'the miners' village'. Most activity had ceased by the 1930s and the remains have lain relatively undisturbed ever since. In order to reach the valley from Coniston it is necessary to turn directly up the road at the side of the Black Bull and continue up the hill, through a fell gate where the road becomes an unsurfaced track. Soon a deep ravine can be seen on the left containing the Church Beck as it tumbles through pools and boulders forming the Coniston Waterfalls. Further along the track, past Miners' Bridge and the Youth Hostel, which once housed the Mine manager, a complex of terraces, ruined buildings and walls form the old Bonsor Dressing Floors.

The site owes its appearance to the work carried out in the mid-nineteenth century. The whole area is fascinating: wheel pits, dressing mills and heaps of spoil abound, as do the fine arched portals of adits leading straight into the hillsides. Beware, many are unsafe.

The main sources of ore were the Bonsor and Paddy End veins. Overlooked by the scree-pocked face of Old Man of Coniston are clusters of workings with intriguing names such as Thriddle Foot, God's Blessing, Black Scar, Sam's Bottom and Simon's Nick, the latter after a legendary miner who sold his soul to the devil for a few extra coppers. The whole area is fascinating: the remains of wheel pits, dressing mills and heaps of spoil abound, peppered with old engine shafts and tunnels leading straight into the hillside. Beware! Many of the clefts and levels have false floors concealing stopes falling over 100 feet (33 metres). That one of the levels is known as 'hospital' is perhaps no coincidence. The mind boggles at the huge labours involved to extract the precious copper ore from here, so far from the main road at lake level. It is known that aerial ropeways were used as transport, powered by stream-fed water-wheels, of which many wheel pits remain.

Now quiet and free from the hustle and bustle of earlier times, the whole area makes an extremely interesting walk, but care must be taken not to fall foul of potential dangers – loose stones and masonry and the beckoning tunnels. Anyone seriously contemplating exploring underground would be well advised to obtain a copy of Eric Holland's excellent field guide and proceed with extreme caution.

General Information

Owner: South Lakeland District Council
Title: Coniston Copper Mines Valley
Location: Copper Mines Valley, Coniston, Cumbria. Map reference OS sheet 97 290987
Enquiries: Coniston Information Centre
Telephone: 05394 41533
Directions: From Coniston turn directly up the road at the side of the Black Bull. Continue up it, through a fell gate. Pass Coniston Waterfalls on the left, and the Youth Hostel, to reach the mines area.
Access: Any reasonable time
Nearest car park: Coniston
Distance: 1.5 miles (2.4 kilometres)
Time to explore: Three hours
Conditions: Open fell country; stout footwear is recommended. Always beware of unfenced shafts and unstable masonry.
Facilities: None, but good picnic and rough walking area.

Standedge Canal Tunnel

Contrary to popular belief it was water and coal, not steam, that was the driving force behind the Industrial Revolution. Water powered the cotton mills that had been built to exploit the mechanical ingenuity of the newly invented machines like the 'Spinning Jenny', perfected by James Hargreaves in 1764, and Richard Arkwright's spinning frame of 1769 which produced cotton thread strong enough to be used as a warp in machine looms. And as the mills increased in number and spread up the valleys of Lancashire and Derbyshire, towns began to grow around them. Workers forsook the land and became 'townies', where, deprived of facilities for wood-gathering, they looked to coal to provide fuel for cooking and keeping warm in winter. But Tyne sea-coal, while it could be shipped quite easily around the creeks and rivers of the east coast, was prohibitively expensive to cart overland and, although inland collieries sprang up to meet the demand, roads were so appalling that transport was restricted to the poor, over-worked pack-horse or the river. And rivers had a nasty habit of never flowing where you wanted to go. A pack-horse was hard pushed to carry more than a few hundred-weight over any reasonable distance, yet the same animal could haul 50 tons with ease if the load was afloat; clearly the answer lay in the canal.

Canals had been used by the Romans who linked the Witham and the Trent with the Fosdyke. Never a race to make hasty decisions, the stoic British gave the matter due consider-

Continued overleaf

ation and put off building their first true canal, the Exeter, until 1566. There was then a further gap of two-hundred years before the first 'modern' canal was constructed at St Helens in 1757, to be followed four years later by the innovative and aptly named Duke of Bridgewater's Canal. Designed to carry coal to Manchester from the Duke's mines at Worsley, its construction was supervised by James Brindley and necessitated the building of a 200 yard (182 metre) long aqueduct over the river Irwell, a feat of engineering that was to set the standard for subsequent navigators for well over a century and firmly established Brindley as the 'canal man'.

Brindley also pioneered the tunnel as a way of overcoming difficult topography. Until he started building the Harecastle Tunnel on his Trent and Mersey Canal, no one in Britain had seriously attempted tunneling right through a hillside. Started in 1766 this 1.6 mile (2.6 kilometre) construction took eleven years to excavate; too long for James Brindley who sadly died before its completion. But where he dared to tread, others soon followed and as a result, some of the greatest works of canal navigation remain largely hidden from view.

The longest tunnel on any British waterway occurs at Marsden on the Huddersfield Narrow Canal, a 'cut' which joined Sir John Ramsden's Broad Canal in Huddersfield with the Ashton Canal in Manchester, the third of the trans-Pennine navigations. Opened in 1811, Standedge Tunnel, with its passing places and ventilation shafts, cost the then colossal sum of £160,000 to bore under Saddleworth Moor, making it the most expensive canal tunnel in Britain, and, at 656 feet (200 metres) above sea level, also the highest. Over 3 miles (4,900 metres) in length, the 9 feet (2.7 metres) wide tunnel had 9 feet of headroom above water-level, all of which had to be hacked and blasted out of the tough local gritstone. It used to take three and a half hours for boats to be legged through; bearing in mind the jagged state of the walls and roof, wear and tear on boot-leather must have been phenomenal.

But the canal was never a major commercial success and when the company found the competition from the Huddersfield and Manchester Railway too much to contend with, they sold out in 1844. The railway engineers made full use of the canal tunnel for their construction work, cutting galleries through at intervals for the purpose of access, drainage and ventilation and when, three years later, the first train puffed under the melancholy moor it added insult to injury by filling the old water-course with steam. Nevertheless, despite the seventy-four locks, canal traffic continued until 1905, by which time the cost of maintenance was exceeding receipts. Apart from a short section in Huddersfield, the canal was abandoned in 1944.

To find the north portal of Standedge from Marsden Station turn left to the Junction Inn. A lane leads to the British Waterways Board maintenance yard and from a bridge over the canal it is possible to view the portal with the two disused single track railway tunnels above it and a double-track tunnel still in use. The south portal is at Diggle. The date on the keystone, 1893, refers to an extension necessitated by alterations to the nearby railway. As the tunnel is part water-conduit and also serves to drain the railway tunnels it has been quite well maintained, but access is strictly only for British Waterways engineers.

General Information

Owner: British Waterways Board
Title: Standedge Tunnel
Location: Marsden, West Yorkshire
Enquiries: British Waterways Board, Skipton Section Office
Telephone: 0274 611303
Directions: North portal: facing Marsden Station turn left to the Junction Inn and follow the lane to the British Waterways maintenance yard. The portal is visible from the nearby canal bridge. South portal: turn off the A62 and proceed to Diggle.
Access: Strictly not open to the public
Nearest car park: Marsden Station
Distance: 440 yards (400 metres)
Time to explore: Half an hour
Conditions: Metalled roads throughout
Facilities: None. The usual facilities are available at the Junction Inn.

Stump Cross Caverns

Like the many of natural caves found in this hinterland region of Britain, the cave system of which Stump Cross Caverns is a part was discovered when miners accidentally broke into a section of the caves when prospecting for lead, in 1858. Whilst not a particularly unusual event in itself, it was rare to find a cave with such outstandingly rich and ancient stalactite and stalagmite formations, some of which have been scientifically dated as being at least 300,000 years old. It would appear that the caves themselves were effectively sealed by debris during the last Ice Age so it is doubtful if prehistoric man ever gained access, but there is ample evidence of local Stone Age settlements, one of which has been carbon dated at around 4,500 BC.

It is reasonable to assume that lead mining was being carried out in the surrounding hills, possibly even during the Romano–British period. Certainly it took place in medieval times, but major mining activities did not really get under way until the late seventeenth century. Although the Pennine lead mining industry extended right into the beginning of the present century, the most intense period of mining took place in the early 1800s during the time when the price of lead was buoyant. From the late 1600s, therefore, the economic history of Stumps Cross has been closely interwoven with the prosperity or otherwise of the local lead mining industry. Mineral veins abounded and often outcropped on limestone points in the area. At one time the area must have seemed a positive hive of industry in comparison with today, the local centre being at nearby Greenhow, a village standing about 1,310 feet (400 metres) above sea level and claiming to have the highest church in the British Isles, topographically speaking.

The miners who first broke into the cave inadvertently found themselves in what proved to be the most scenic part of the system, consisting of about 875 yards (800 metres) of accessible caverns. They could not have realized that a further 4 miles (6 kilometres) of water-sculpted passageways lay beneath their feet. The present owners therefore effectively operate a two level strategy: Level One is the show cave open to members of the public, and Level Two is reserved for the serious speleological researcher and for potholers. The show cave is floodlit and dry and has sections known as Jewel Box, Snow Drift, Chamber of Pillars, Policeman's Truncheon and Wedding Cake, all of which are named after the more eye-catching formations to be found there. Only recently opened to the public, the Wolverine Cave, an immensely decorative tributary of the main cave, boasts not only finds of the bones of wolverine, bison, wolf and reindeer, but also the site of rarities such as delicate helictites. As the name suggests these are curious stalactites which apparently defy the laws of gravity. Other items of interest include calcite straws, rimstone pools and, in the final chamber currently open to the public, very unusual and beautiful combinations of coloured stalactites, stalagmites, curtains and pillars.

General Information

Owner: B Gill and G Hanley
Title: Stump Cross Caverns
Location: Greenhow Hill, Pateley Bridge, Harrogate, North Yorkshire. Map reference OS sheet 99 089635
Enquiries: Stump Cross Caverns
Telephone: 0756 752780
Directions: Signposted from Harrogate and Skipton on B6265 on the Pately Bridge–Grassington road
Access: Open daily, April to October 10 a.m.–6 p.m., November to March 10 a.m.–5.30 p.m. and winter weekends 11 a.m.–4 p.m.
Nearest car park: Ample free car/coach parking on site
Distance: 22 yards (20 metres)
Time to explore: 45 minutes
Conditions: Dry graded gravel footpaths throughout. The roof is low in places. There is a flight of 70 steps. The caves are unsuitable for the severely disabled.
Facilities: Café serving hot and cold snacks, confectionery and ice cream; gift shop, lavatories. Potholing by arrangement.
Parties: School and coach parties welcome.

Tilberthwaite Mine – Penny Rigg Copper Mill

The Coniston area is dotted with abandoned copper and slate mines which succumbed to old age, cheap imported copper or lack of adequate financial backing. Mining seems to have begun in the area in the early seventeenth century and continued until the beginning of the Second World War. For the most part the mines are ruins and the shafts and levels better avoided, although there are exceptions. Should the reader seriously feel they just must venture into an abandoned mine working or their experience of life will be incomplete, a study of the possibilities on offer at Penny Rigg is well worth looking into, literally.

The Greenburn and Tilberthwaite Mining Company was one of the last such undertakings to close down. Penny Rigg Copper Mill was linked into Tilberthwaite by a 3,280 feet (1,000 metre) level known as Horse Crag, or more strictly Tilberthwaite Deep Adit, which drained the workings and, in this case, served the useful purpose of being a convenient route along which to bring ore, from the deep veins under the hill, to the treatment plant. If you take sensible precautions it is not even absolutely essential to don overalls, a pair of stout rubber boots, preferably with the steel toe-caps, and old trousers, will do. It is, however, essential to carry sensible lighting with a back-up of some sort should one source fail. Don't rely on matches or candles!

When you arrive at Penny Rigg Mill large spoil heaps and old mine buildings can be seen to the left of the road. The spoil heaps consist mostly of slate waste and some hint of its metalliferous content may be deduced from the brown stains exhibited by these piles of scrap slate and mining rubble.

The entrance to Deep Adit can be found in the lowest of a series of slate quarries and nestles in a scar covered with small trees and ferns. The dark, cool tunnel is silent and eerie, the eeriness accentuated by the hollow drip, drip, drip of tiny droplets of water from the roof. It is not at all welcoming, having a certain distinct chill about it. That it contains one foot (a third of a metre) of water in places is only to put off the timid. Equipped with a mining lamp or waterproof lantern, and a similarly enthusiastic companion, the partially flooded passage is perfectly navigable. With the aid of a stout stick to probe the hidden bottom, it is possible to wade the length of the passage.

Presently the tunnel opens up into a sizeable cavern seemingly large enough to contain a church. This is a 'closehead' the local term for an underground slate working. Incidentally, the cavern has nothing whatsoever to do with copper, slate having been extracted from here by John 'Willie' Shaw, who, together with two other assistants worked this portion of Horse Crag level, until he was forced to retire due to his great age. Compressed air for their drills was provided by a creaking and rusty old paraffin compressor. It is probable that they only worked here during the months of winter – a neat way of keeping warm during a lakeland freeze. At about 200 yards (180 metres) from daylight, the lengthy tunnel is blocked by fallen clay, but it is reasonably safe to proceed to this point.

Tilberthwaite Deep is pretty small beer to those whose main aim in life is to set new underground endurance records or prove the legend that the mines in Matlock are linked subterraneously with the caves of Cheddar and the Vale of Avalon, but as a beginner's unguided trip into the unknown it passes a pleasant hour or so in equally pleasant surroundings.

General Information

Owner: South Lakeland District Council
Title: Tilberthwaite Deep Adit
Location: Yewdale, Cumbria. Map reference OS sheet 90 306007
Enquiries: Coniston Information Centre
Telephone: 05394 41533
Directions: To reach Penny Rigg, follow the Ambleside road out of Coniston, turning left at the road to Tilberthwaite Gill. Pass over the cattle-grid and soon large spoil heaps and old mine buildings can be seen to the left of the road.
Access: Any reasonable time
Nearest car park: In adjoining lane
Distance: 275 yards (250 metres)

Time to explore: One hour
Conditions: Open fell country. Access to mine necessitates wading along a partially flooded tunnel. Waterproof boots and

protective headgear and suitable illumination are essential. Always beware of unfenced shafts and unstable masonry.
Facilities: None, but good picnic and walking area.

White Scar Caves

Situated at a height of 820 feet (250 metres) above sea level, within the Yorkshire Dales National Park, and set in the steep, deeply scarred limestone valley of Chapel-le-Dale, White Scar Caves provide the visitor with a feast of visual experiences from truly beautiful stalactite and stalagmite formations to underground streams and waterfalls. Again for the most part carved out of the Great Scar limestone by countless millennia of aqueous erosion dating from the Great Ice Ages, the caves neatly sit astride the Craven Fault, evidence of which can be seen in the entrance tunnel. The caves lay hidden until they were discovered in 1923 by the intrepid Christopher Long who, chancing upon an entrance, proceeded to make a solo exploration deep into the cave, largely on his hands and knees, later reporting back his discoveries to the owners. This foolhardy act prompted the blasting of an access tunnel enabling the caves to be opened up to tourists.

The great incentive for this display of enthusiasm was the fact that far from being a dry cave, White Scar contains running water, a great deal of it after heavy rains. So much so that the guides use a pet piece of flowstone to monitor the level in bad weather – it takes seven hours for rain to percolate into the cave system and it can then be up to the roof in three hours!

There are few places open to the public in Britain which give the visitor such a graphic impression of the part played by the action of water in the formation of caves. Soon after entering the main cave, the sound of rushing water, from the first of two waterfalls, can be heard booming through the labyrinth, filling the air with noise and making conversation difficult. Passing alongside the boulder-strewn stream bed and through passages decorated with coloured flowstone, the visitor then

reaches a section in which the pavement gives way to a timber board-walk, with again the sound of running water, for at this point the stream is directly underfoot, no doubt further deepening the passage as it has done for thousands of years.

The second waterfall is even more impressive. On reaching the top of a tall chamber, the stream plummets, resounding off shimmering walls of wet rock and crashing into the pool below. Strong natural colours abound, caused by impurities in the rock including iron, lead, manganese and traces of copper. The ensuing passages are sumptuously decorated with flowstone, stalactite, stalagmite and gour pools. Being very much a 'natural' cave in which the process of formation is steadily progressing all around, the part of the complex seen by the public represents a mere fraction of what lies further into the Scar. Groups wishing to do so can choose an adventure caving expedition which will take them beyond the floodlights, far into the deeper recesses of the caves. White Scar Caves have been officially designated a site of Special Scientific Interest, so that the natural cave environment is protected for scientific research and for the benefit of future generations.

General Information

Owner: White Scar Caves Ltd
Title: White Scar Caves
Location: Yorkshire Dales National Park, Yorkshire. Map reference OS sheet 98 714747
Enquiries: The Manager, White Scar Caves Ltd, Ingleton, via Carnforth, Lancashire
Telephone: 05242 41244
Directions: 1.5 miles (2.4 kilometres) from Ingleton on B6255
Access: Open daily, March to November, 10 a.m.–4.30 p.m. April to September, 10 a.m.–6.30 p.m. Closed December, January and February.
Nearest car park: Ample free car/coach parking on site
Distance: 55 yards (50 metres)
Time to explore: 45 minutes

Continued overleaf

Yorkshire Mining Museum

At the Yorkshire Mining Museum they have taken down the 'keep out' boards and put up a welcome sign so that everyone with a desire to go underground can experience life at the coal face as it was in the 1800s and right up to the present day. Caphouse Colliery made a valuable contribution to the coal production of Yorkshire from 1790 up until its closure in 1985. Now a major face-lift has made the colliery the centrepiece of this fascinating and educational mining museum. Mining is still one of Yorkshire's basic industries and much of Britain's industrial growth was fueled by coal, yet, until recently, few outside the industry had the opportunity to wander around a pit-head let alone go underground to see and understand something of the miner's life and its complexities.

The main exhibition is Caphouse Colliery itself. At its core is the stone engine house and old timber headstock, both of which were erected in 1876. The winding engine is the original twin-cylinder Davy Brothers steam winder unit supplied when the pit-head was originally erected, while the Head Gear is thought to be the last one made of wood still surviving in Yorkshire, and was in regular use until 1974. But, intriguingly enough, the oldest feature of the pit is not a building but the main shaft itself. This was marked on a map dated 1795 and thus may well be the oldest usable shaft of any British coal mine, perhaps the oldest one in Europe.

The other buildings provide a good indication of the pace of the modernization programmes that have taken place over the years, culminating in a drift driven in 1971, after which coal was brought to the surface by conveyor, rendering shaft-hauling obsolete. Near to the mine complex are bell-pits which date from the very earliest days of mining and a horse gin, used to wind coal, men and materials up and down the mine before the coming of steam power, when the industrial revolution was in its infancy.

Outcrop mining was widespread from comparatively early times in the hills west of Wakefield, where the Yorkshire coalfield reaches the surface. Certainly there is evidence that coal was being mined at Flockton as far back as 1515; by the seventeenth century cast-iron, coal-burning ranges were a common sight in local homes. But as there were no large towns in the vicinity and only pack-horse transport available, production was only carried out on a small scale for local consumption until the eighteenth century, by which time the West Riding towns were growing fast and were hungry for coal. In 1769 canalization made the Calder navigation accessible from Horbury Bridge, enabling local coal to be distributed economically all over the country, thereby encouraging mining development throughout the area, Caphouse being one such pit.

As part of the museum tour, visitors have the opportunity to travel 460 feet (140 metres) down the Caphouse Colliery main shaft to the New Hards Seam. The underground tour lasts about an hour. After lamping up, ex-miners guide the visitor through reconstructions of the difficult and potentially dangerous world of the face worker where life-like scenes recreate the days before mechanization when coal was cut by muscle-power alone. Here it can be seen how children worked down the mines closing ventilation doors and hauling coal along wooden roadways lined with pit props.

At the modern coal-face visitors are confronted by the monstrous machines which, until comparatively recently, filled the tunnels with ear-shattering noise and stifling dust. Back on the surface there are exhibits of modern machinery, including vast coal-cutters. By far the most impressive, not to say terrifying, of these is the Dosco Road Header, designed to swing the most fearful and enormous rotary cutting blades at the coal-face to gouge out roadways in modern mines. You can also say hello to Able the pit pony, visit the pit-head baths or take a ride on a haulage railway.

General Information

Owners: Yorkshire Mining Museum Trust
Title: Yorkshire Mining Museum Caphouse Colliery
Location: New Road, Overton, Wakefield, Yorkshire
Enquiries: Commercial Manager, Yorkshire Mining Museum
Telephone: 0924 848806
Directions: The museum stands on the A642 Huddersfield to Wakefield road.

Access: Open daily, 10 a.m.–5 p.m. Closed for Christmas and New Year.
Nearest car park: Ample free car/coach parking on site.
Distance: 55 yards (50 metres)
Time to explore: Three hours minimum.
Conditions: Dry graded footpaths throughout. Protective headgear and miners' lamps are provided free. Warm clothing and stout footwear are recommended. The museum is committed to allowing disabled access wherever possible. Please discuss requirements with the staff in advance.
Facilites: Licensed cafeteria serving hot and cold snacks, confectionery and ice cream; gift shop selling a wide range of books and souvenirs; picnic area; lavatories. Museum; audio-visual theatre. Displays showing the history of the Yorkshire Coalfield. Displays of mining machinery. A schools/group private study room is available on request. The museum caters for group evening visits by special arrangement. A full catering service can be provided if required for children or adults. Prebooking is essential.
Parties: School and coach parties are welcome but please make group bookings well in advance.

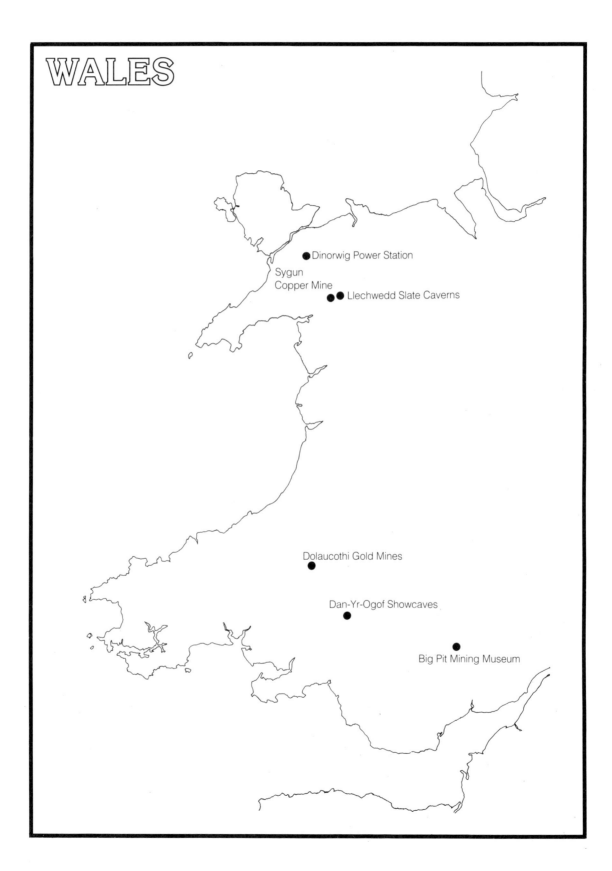

WALES

Dinorwig Power Station

Sygun
Copper Mine
Llechwedd Slate Caverns

Dolaucothi Gold Mines

Dan-Yr-Ogof Showcaves

Big Pit Mining Museum

Welsh copper, Welsh slate, Welsh gold, Welsh coal and Welsh electricity; it makes you wonder where we would be without our favourite principality. Starting in the north, in the shadow of the rugged mass of Snowdon and surrounded by the spectacular scenery of the Snowdon National Park, Dinorwig is perhaps the most awe inspiring location in this entire book, judged both externally and internally. Can you imagine that, buried in the heart of the Cambrian Mountains, totally hidden from view, there is a power station that could, if necessary, at the touch of a remote micro-switch, turn on something approaching 1,750,000 horse power in ten seconds flat? All this is in a series of underground chambers that give the impression that they could swallow Cardiff Arms Park at a single gulp.

Beddgelert, on the opposite side of Snowdon, in the gorgeous Gwynant Valley, on the mountain route to Royal Caernarfon, is again right at the centre of probably the most popular tourist area in Wales. Opened relatively recently, the Sygun Copper Mine has already attracted thousands of visitors keen to experience the magic and fascination of nineteenth-century metal mining. The slate caverns at Llechwedd, on the other hand, have been open to the public since 1972, over which time some three million visitors, including members of both the British and Japanese royal families, have seen where slates for some of the world's most prestigious roofs first started out.

The National Trust's very own gold mines at Dolaucothi near Pumpsaint are said to have been in existence for nearly 2,000 years. Set amidst the wooded hillsides of the beautiful Cothi Valley you can wander at will along ancient miners' trails or see for yourselves the only place in Britain where the Romans mined for gold. The Dan-yr-Ogof Centre, in the Brecon Beacons National Park, has won more awards than we have space to mention. The showcaves are rightly famous, both for their sheer size and for what they have to offer – everything from a gentle Sunday afternoon saunter with the family through the cathedral-like spaces of the largest show caves in Britain, to the danger and excitement of 'rough' adventure caving for the serious enthusiast.

Last, but by no means least, a guide to the underground wonders of Wales would not be complete without Big Pit. The tightly knit loyalty and community spirit of the South Wales mining villages is almost as legendary as the stoicism and camaraderie of the miners themselves. With modern mining methods and a Coal Board that tends to favour the arguments of accountants rather than miners, traditional mining centres like Blaenafon are dying out fast. Big Pit was only just saved from terminal 'landscaping' in the nick of time. Now, thanks largely due to the enthusiasm of the local mining community who wanted something left behind to show for all those generations of hard, back-breaking work, visitors can go down a 'real' coal mine on a unique underground tour in the pleasant company of the man who knows more about mining than anyone – an ex-miner.

Big Pit Mining Museum

Standing as it does on the eastern rim of the South Wales coal measures which outcrop on the hills of the surrounding area, Big Pit is one of the last of the typical traditional Welsh coal mines. An important factor influencing the history of Big Pit and the collieries that once surrounded it is that, in addition to coal measures, there were also raw materials available locally for the making of iron, namely copious quantities of ironstone and limestone. In 1789 three adventurers from Staffordshire opened an iron smelting furnace at Blaenafon. Across the valley from Big Pit the remains of these works are currently in the process of being preserved. Because the coal outcropped on the hillsides, the early mines at Blaenafon were in the form of levels or drifts, following the sloping seams into the hillside. After a century of active life and having survived a succession of Coal Board closures which resulted in Big Pit being the only operational mine in the area, in 1980 it too ceased production, curiously enough almost exactly 100 years after it opened.

Although many ancillary sections of Big Pit never survived the close down, such vital buildings as the Lamp Room, the Tram Circuit, Pit Top and the Winder House are still much the same as the day when mining stopped. So too is the old Blacksmith's Shop, one of the most important installations at Big Pit; before mechanization, virtually all the tools and equipment used in the mine were made on the premises. Three of the nine forges are still intact whilst outside in the yard are stables for three horses, complete with cast iron mangers made at the local ironworks.

Dominating the whole site is the main Pit Head Gear where the underground part of the tour commences. Amidst the hustle and bustle of the cage area the intrepid visitor is kitted out with helmet and miner's lamp and asked to surrender contraband – anything that might be a fire risk, including digital watches. With the sound of bells ringing in the ears you are lowered gently down the 300 feet (91 metres) shaft to Pit Bottom. From here, in the authentic directional beams of cap lamps, the heavy old wooden ventilation doors, once operated by boys and girls working twelve-hour shifts, bang shut and you are back in Victorian Britain amongst pit props and underground stables where dozens of pit-ponies with names like Dragon, Prince, Victor and Irish awaited their turn to haul heavy trains of coal, rarely seeing the light of day. Miners had to buy the ponies themselves, so if 'pony were killed were 'ell to pay'. Then there are the coal faces where, in the nineteenth century, whole families worked in the dusty darkness. Husbands and fathers hewed with pick and shovel while women and children loaded the cruel black coal into baskets, barrows and later 'trams' with their bare hands and hauled them to Pit Bottom. Here too from a later time, are the massive flameproof winders which took much of the backache but little of the danger out of mining. Finally, the return trip passes through the two-centuries-old ironstone workings.

The guides, all miners themselves, learnt the reality of pit-life the hard way. With their stoic cheerfulness they help to bring the Big Pit to life and make the visit a memorable experience. Back at the surface the Pit Head Baths should not on any account be missed. Prior to their construction in 1936, paid for by the miners out of their wages, men had to go home dressed in working clothes and their own dirt. The complex contains baths, locker room and a canteen which is still in use and also houses a display consisting of an excellent selection of photographs telling the miner's story. Lastly there is a typical miner's cottage of the 1930s and an excellent museum. It has to be remembered that Big Pit did not exist in isolation, it was the workplace of hundreds of men who, with their families, ate, drank, sported, worshipped, lived and died in the nearby town of Blaenafon and its companion village of Forgeside. The spirits of the old miners must now rest more easily, knowing that their pit is being lovingly looked after.

General Information

Owner: Big Pit Blaenafon Trust
Title: Big Pit Mining Museum
Location: Blaenafon, Gwent
Enquiries: The Mine Manager
Telephone: 0495 790311
Directions: From Pontypool take the A4043 to Blaenafon after which Big Pit is well signposted.
Access: Open daily 10 a.m.–5 p.m. Last trip underground 3.30 p.m. During the months of January and February it is advisable to telephone for details.
Nearest car park: Ample free car/coach parking on site.
Distance: 55 yards (50 metres) to the Visitor Centre.
Time to explore: One hour below ground. Three hours minimum for the entire complex.

Conditions: Dry graded footpaths throughout. Stout footwear and warm clothing is recommended. Protective headgear and miners' lamps are provided free. Special facilities available for the disabled by prior arrangement. Please discuss requirements with the Visitor Centre.
Facilities: Original Miners' Canteen offering a range of meals, hot and cold snacks, confectionery and ice cream; gift shop selling a wide range of books and souvenirs; picnic area; lavatories; museum. Original colliery buildings including Blacksmith's Shop, Steam Winding Engine House, Pit Head Baths and clothes lockers, Lamp Room. Reconstruction of typical 1930s miner's cottage. Giant photomontage of Welsh mining valley scenes. Museum of mining artefacts. Big Pit steam railway (operated by the Pontypool and Blaenafon Railway Society).
Parties: School and coach parties welcome but only by prior arrangement please.

Dan-Yr-Ogof Showcaves

Dan-Yr-Ogof is the largest of a series of caves lying in the magnificent Upper Tawe Valley, south of the Brecon Beacons. The Showcave was first comprehensively explored by the Morgan Brothers in 1912. Present day visitors no longer have to go through the indignity of crawling on their stomachs or fording underground lakes in a tiny coracle as did this intrepid pair, because wide pathways have been cut to circumnavigate the defiles. The tour of the cave is a long one and winds through a series of convoluted natural tunnels, taking in such features as the Frozen Waterfall, Pencil Column, Dagger Chamber and most remarkable of all, the Cauldron Chamber. Here a magnificent 18 feet (5.5 metre) curtain can be seen suspended high above the pathway. This is the largest flowstone curtain known in any British show cave. Further on the percussive sound of falling water of an underground river heralds the presence of the Cascades, the Lakes and the Parting of the Ways which leads back to the open air.

Climbing up the hill, where owls, buzzards and kestrels hunt amongst the crags, past the intriguing park full of fibre-glass dinosaurs, which also gives access to the Bone Cave, we come to the second major attraction of the complex, the aptly named Cathedral Cave. This enormous cave features a series of dioramas including one very telling study depicting the Morgan Brothers, attired in casual outdoor country clothes, including flat hats, exploring in their primitive coracle. The final surprise is the huge cavern which opens up at the rear of the cave system and from which it takes its name. It really is vast, dwarfing the figures which represent members of the South Wales Caving Club clambering down rope ladders through the midst of crashing waterfalls.

General Information

Owner: Dan-Yr-Ogof Showcaves Ltd
Title: Dan-Yr-Ogof Showcave
Location: Abercrave (Abercraf), Glyntawe, Swansea, West Glamorgan
Enquiries: The Manager
Telephone: 0639 730284
Directions: Situated in the Brecon Beacons National Park on the A4067, midway between Swansea and Brecon.
Access: Open daily, April to October 10 a.m.–5 p.m.
Nearest car park: Ample free car/coach parking on site.
Distance: 55 yards (50 metres) to Visitor Centre
Time to explore: Two hours
Conditions: Dry smooth footpaths throughout. The Showcave contains a series of short flights of steps. The Cathedral Cave has a level concrete floor. The caves are suitable for the more adventurous disabled. Visitors with wheelchairs wishing to see the Showcave please give prior notice.
Facilities: Showcave, Cathedral Cave and Bone Cave. Restaurant and covered picnic area; lavatories; motel and chalet accommodation; museum and audio-visual centre; information centre; dinosaur park; treasure hunt; beginners' spotter pack; adventure caving for beginners and experts.
Parties: Educational parties by arrangement.

Dinorwig Power Station

Situated almost opposite the Snowdon Mountain Railway terminus at Llanberris, Dinorwig Power Station must rank as one of the world's marvels of engineering and construction and yet probably few people taking the famous rack and pinion train up Wales's highest mountain ever give it a thought. Hardly surprising really since it happens to be almost totally underground. Dinorwig utilizes the principle of pumped storage, using the kinetic energy of water falling from an upper reservoir to produce electricity via a turbo-generator. These generators can also operate in reverse, allowing water used in generating mode to be pumped back into the high level reservoir at night using excess power from the national grid when the prime cost of the electricity is relatively low. For this reason Dinorwig has been described as the largest battery in Europe. Demand for electricity fluctuates throughout the day and the peak period demands have to be met quickly and efficiently. Dinorwig provides instant 'on-demand' power and has the fastest response of any power station in the world; it is able to provide 1800 megawatts of electricity from standby within just ten seconds! From complete shutdown it takes a lot longer – all of one and half minutes. And if the main grid should ever fail there are two big diesel generators on hand to provide enough electricity to start up the system.

At reception there is an Exhibition Centre with a permanently mounted photographic display together with a video film showing the project in various stages of construction. There is also a most informative schematic montage which gives the layman a graphic illustration of the pumped storage principle in operation. Because the station itself is far underground, transport is laid on to take visitors the 820 yards (750 metres) to the machinery hall. From the bus it is difficult to imagine that there are a further 3 miles (5 kilometres) of tunnels carrying water between the high and low level reservoirs.

Once the station is reached the sheer scale of the project comes as something of a shock; it is truly stupendous. In order to house all the equipment a cavern was blasted out of the heart of the mountain big enough to swallow up a building the volume of St Paul's Cathedral twice over. Lifts within the main cavern take the visitor to different levels. Upstream of the six turbines, in their own huge chamber, are the six main inlet valves, one for each turbo-generator set. The balance weights alone for these massive rotary monsters total 31.5 tons (32 tonnes) per unit; they need to be fairly hefty, working against a head of 1,755 feet (535 metres). Hearing one open for the first time at close quarters, unleashing something like 65 cubic yards (50 cubic metres) of water a second, is quite an unforgettable experience.

The sound of machinery is everywhere. In the main machinery cavern the vertically-mounted Francis turbines which are on load whirl away below the generator-motors at 500 revolutions per minute, driving them clockwise to generate and being driven by them anti-clockwise when pumping. Rated at 313 megawatts they produce electricity at 18,000 volts. High on one wall above the vast machinery floor is the main control room. From here the whole complex is controlled automatically and a single operator can attend to all six units. In yet another vast vault humming with electricity, a row of step-up transformers raises the output to 400 kilovolts for transmission by water-cooled underground cables to the national grid sub-station at Pentir.

The added expense of underground power cables is but one instance of the CEGB's concern for the environment of this popular national park. Outside a great effort has been made to preserve, protect and enhance the visual amentities of the area for the benefit of both the inhabitants of Llanberris and the tourists. Particular care has been taken to ensure that the tailworks intake/outfall has been sympathetically blended in with the scenery of the old Dinorwig slate quarry which forms a majestic backdrop to the facility. The new dams required were built from local slate and landscaped with indigenous grasses and heather. New roads were carefully routed and the administration building constructed from reclaimed material from the quarry. But for a hole in the hillside no one would know there was a power station there at all.

General Information

Owner: Central Electricity Generating Board
Title: Dinorwig Power Station
Location: Llanberris, near Caernarfon, Gwynedd. Map reference OS sheet 115 593600
Enquiries: Visitor Centre

Telephone: 0286 870935
Directions: Opposite Snowdon Mountain Railway
Access: Currently only by appointment through the Visitor Centre
Nearest car park: Ample free car/coach parking on site
Distance: 55 yards (50 metres)
Time to explore: Video film followed by conducted tour, total two hours.
Conditions: Transport is provided to and from the underground complex. Protective clothing is not required. Protective headgear is provided free. There is a certain amount of machinery noise.
Facilities: Visitor centre display showing stages of construction and schematic operation in montage. Cinema showing video film of project. Transport to underground complex. Guided walking tour around station. Special facilities available for the disabled by prior arangement. Please discuss requirements with the Visitor Centre.
Parties: Group tours for parties of up to seventy-five people by arrangement with the Visitor Centre.

Dolaucothi Gold Mines

The search for metals is said to be one of the principal reasons behind the Roman invasion of Britain. They came to this part of Wales a generation or so after the conquest of southern Britain and established a small fort at Pumpsaint. In the main their interest was in the more utilitarian ores of tin, copper, lead and iron, but no doubt they were not against taking home the odd nugget of Welsh gold if they happened to come across any. Whether they did or not is a matter of some conjecture. Dolaucothi is said to be the only location in these islands where the Romans mined for gold. The theory is that one of their eagle-eyed contingent noticed a sparkling vein of white quartz in the side of the local stream and drew it to the attention of a Roman engineer familiar with gold mining in Spain. Roman or not, someone with plenty of determination cut into the sides and bottom of the valley, excavating a huge pit. From there they evidently followed the gold underground, tunnelling downwards using fire and water to crack the rock. The veins were narrow so their mining activities left behind a series of slots which can still be seen at Mitchell Pit Two.

Close to the quarry are two access tunnels or adits driven into the hillside. Known as the Upper and Lower Roman Adits, they exhibit very distinctive sections: one is coffin shaped and the other square. They were cut entirely by hand using hammers and wedges to split the rock-face, picks and shovels to break it up and hand baskets to carry out the ore and rubble. The roof and sides of the tunnels are smoothly finished, very characteristic of features found in Spain where Romans are known to have employed a similar hand-mining technique. However, this is no guarantee that the tunnels are Roman; mining methods did not materially change until the advent of black powder and straw fuses.

Surprisingly, it appears that prior to the mid-nineteenth century, visitors to the mines were completely unaware that gold had ever been extracted at Dolaucothi, the presence of the precious metal having only been rediscovered in 1844. In 1853 three enthusiastic Australians arrived and set up a water-powered five stamp mill, but their success was not auspicious. In the latter part of the nineteenth century the South Wales Gold Mining Company was formed, but little gold was produced and it was not until 1905 that James Mitchell was employed to re-establish mining in the area. A Cornishman with experience in South Africa, his expertise proved profitable.

It is Mitchell's Adit which provides the subject of the guided tour, and incidentally features a most extraordinary example of sym-

Continued overleaf

biosis, in which a combination of fungus and bacteria can be seen eating into the rock and leeching pure gold. If the process could be harnessed commercially who knows what riches could be extracted from the living rock?

Although named after James Mitchell who supervised mining at Dolaucothi from 1906 to 1911, the adit in fact dates from the late 1880s. Five levels all converge at one point and standing at this underground junction can be quite unnerving as the 'floor' is almost entirely wooden and saturated with water. But have no fear; there is so much arsenic present that wet rot is a biological impossibility!

General Information

Owner: National Trust
Title: Dolaucothi Gold Mines
Location: Pumpsaint, Llanwrda, Dyfed
Enquiries: Project Manager
Telephone: 05585 359
Directions: Signposted from Pumpsaint on the A482 Lampeter to Llanwrda road.
Access: Surface facilities open daily, Easter to October, 10 a.m.–5 p.m. Mine open daily from Whitsun to October.
Nearest car park: Ample free car/coach parking on site
Distance: 220 yards (200 metres)
Time to explore: Two hours minimum. Underground guided tours one hour.
Conditions: Extensive open hill site necessitates a certain amount of climbing. The mine is unsuitable for the severely disabled. Stout footwear is recommended. Protective headgear and miners' lamps are provided free.
Facilities: Gift shop; snack bar; lavatories; visual display; audio-visual presentation.
Parties: School and coach parties welcome.

Llechwedd Slate Caverns

Llechwedd Slate Caverns have belonged to the Greaves family since the early part of the nineteenth century. First revealed to the public in 1972, they currently offer two quite different journeys of discovery into some of the vast caverns which are the result of 150 years of continuous slate mining. Development dates from 1836 when J W Greaves decided to concentrate his efforts on extracting slate from the area around Blaenau Ffestiniog. This would appear to have been a shrewd move as the Ffestiniog mineral line was just about to open making it possible for vast amounts of slate to be shipped to the new harbour at Porth Madog at a fraction of the cost of pack-pony or horse-drawn cart. Success was by no means instant and Greaves was on the verge of bankruptcy, when, in 1849, he found a workable seam of excellent blue slate, deep below the surface at Llechwedd. The quality proved to be so good that it won him international fame and many prize medals.

The caverns are easily found as they happen to be situated opposite Goddfar Ganol, the world's largest slate mine. On entering the site, the visitor is faced with a choice of two tours. The Miners' Underground Tramway enters the side of the mountain, taking passengers through a succession of spectacular chambers.

Passengers hear a miner explain the workings of the mine and experience sights and sounds which recreate the impression of Victorian mining conditions. The Deep Mine tour begins with a journey down Britain's steepest underground passenger railway in a specially designed 3 ton (3.048 tonne) cable-car. Descending below the level of the upper slate floor, visitors alight at a lower level and, wearing protective helmets, are guided on a voyage of discovery through the maze of tunnels. Successive chambers of ever increasing size reverberate as sound and light presentations, together with tableaux, tell the story of the mine and miners. The climax of the trip takes place in the last of these chambers, all but filled by a huge silent lake. Gradually the visitor becomes aware that the cold, damp underground air is vibrating to the melodious murmur of some distant, Welsh male voice choir. For a moment time seems to stand still as the spine-tingling music swells in perfect harmony, and the melodious voices join together, echoing across the reflections of the limpid blue water just as the voices of countless groups of homing miners must have done many times before.

General Information

Owner: J W Greaves & Sons
Title: Llechwedd Slate Caverns

Continued on page 129

Right
The nineteenth-century
Blacksmith's Shop is still in
working order at
Blaenafon's historic Big Pit
Mining Museum situated
on the eastern rim of the
South Wales coalfield
(page 120)

Below
The lofty Cathedral Cave
at Dan-yr-Ogof features
four cave 'explorers' and
their specialized equipment
(page 121)

A guide explains the unique symbiotic combination of fungus and bacteria busy leeching microscopic quantities of pure Welsh gold from the cold damp rock at ancient Dolaucothi (page 123)

The vast valve hall of Dinorwig Power Station contains the six of these huge main inlet valves which, in emergency, can close under gravity against over a half a million horse power head of water (page 122)

Deep under the Welsh hillside fast growing stalagmites of ferrous oxide and natural ochre stealthily reclaim the worked-out levels at Sygun Copper Mine (page 129)

Llechwedd's stunning underground lake which periodically reverberates to the sounds of the local chapel organ and a Welsh male voice choir (page 124)

A pleasant prospect greets visitors who take the trouble to find their way to the once busy banks of the Edinburgh and Glasgow Union Canal at Falkirk's Low Park (page 133)

The bleak basalt entrance of Fingal's Cave which inspired Mendelssohn to compose his well known 'Hebrides Overture' (page 134) (David Webster of Oban)

Location: Blaenau Ffestiniog, Gwynedd
Enquiries: The General Manager
Telephone: 0766 830306
Directions: Signposted on the A470 between Betws-y-Coed and Dolgellau
Access: Open daily, 10 a.m.–6 p.m. The last tram leaves at 5.15 p.m. in summer and 4.15 p.m. in winter.
Nearest car park: Ample free car/coach parking on site
Distance: 55 yards (50 metres)

Time to explore: Three hours
Conditions: Surface area paved. Level access to underground tramway. Deep mine tour involves descending 61 steps.
Facilities: The Miner's Arms pub serving food and drink; licensed restaurant; café and soup kitchen. Gift shop selling souvenirs, books and sweets. Lavatories including facilities for handicapped persons. Craft demonstrations; video presentations on the history of slate; exhibitions.
Parties: School and coach parties welcome.

Sygun Copper Mine

Copper was one of the first metals to be used by man and has in fact been exploited in North Wales since the Bronze Age. Often the ore-bearing lodes surfaced high up amongst rocky outcrops, staining the rocks and drawing the eye of those early prospectors. Later miners recognized that water was plentiful and could be used for powering crushing machinery and, even more vital, for pumping. This further encouraged exploration of the area for metalliferous lodes that went deeper underground. In just such a situation Sygun Copper Mine was born.

Typically, the workings commenced high on the Welsh mountainside, following the out-cropping ore veins. The lower tunnels were not driven until later on during the eighteenth and nineteenth centuries. Production at Sygun ceased during the early part of the twentieth century and it was not until 1983 that work was started to clear the mine of debris. Finally, in 1986, the mine was opened for the first time as a tourist attraction. Careful restoration work was carried out to preserve the feeling of stepping back into Sygun's Victorian mining heyday and, as such, gives a good idea of the working environment of a nineteenth-century hard rock miner.

Although never a particularly prosperous copper mine, Sygun holds an important place in the industrial heritage of North Wales as, along with Clogau, it was one of the first commercial treatment plants to install Elmore's revolutionary flotation process for the separation of copper sulphides from the mother rock. After a lengthy period of unprofitable operation, Sygun closed in 1903, leaving behind a legacy of back-breaking work and insultingly low wages for the men who risked their lives labouring underground. Some of the chambers have uniquely beautiful, comparatively newly formed ferrous oxide stalactite and stalagmite formations and ochre beds. Such unusual formations are rarely found in areas readily accessible by the public.

The tour begins at the entrance to the deep adit driven in 1830 and each step of the mining process is clearly explained by audio presentations in Welsh, English, French and German. After passing through an area of overhead stoping where ore was removed from a subsidiary vein, the level is partially blocked by a windlass standing guard over the head of a shaft which provided access to lower levels before these became flooded. From this point it is definitely prudent to ascend rather than descend. In the good old days, men had to climb slippery wooden ladders, but now a modern steel stairway leads up to the Victoria level, once reached from further up the mountain, and the main access tunnel to the main lode. Here, inside a huge stope known as the Victoria Chamber, the visitor is treated to a sound and light display presenting some of the many unusual and exciting features to be seen in the mine. Returning to surface it is worth taking the time to walk around the various outside exhibits which include a set of working stamps powered by its own water-wheel. On a fine spring day with the rhododendrons in bloom and the Moel Hebog massif dominating the beautiful Gwynant Valley the prospect is one which is likely to remain in the memory for a long time.

Continued overleaf

General Information

Owner: Mr and Mrs P J Amies
Title: Sygun Copper Mine
Location: Beddgelert, Caernarfon, Gwynedd
Enquiries: Sygun Copper Mine
Telephone: 076686 595
Directions: On the outskirts of Beddgelert on the A498 to Capel Curig
Access: Open daily March to October 10 a.m.–6 p.m. Last tour 5.15 p.m. Reduced hours during October. Open most weekends during winter. Visits on other out-of-season days by arrangement.

Nearest car park: Free car parking on site. Coaches may park in the lay-by adjoining the entrance.
Distance: 110 yards (100 metres)
Time to explore: 45 minutes
Conditions: Moderately dry graded footpaths. There are a total of 186 steps in four separate flights. The upper levels of the mine are unsuitable for the severely disabled. Stout footwear is recommended.
Facilities: Gift shop selling souvenirs, sweets, chocolates, hot and cold drinks and light refreshments; bookstall; lavatories. British Tourist Authority Award winner. Video show of historic aspects of local mining.
Parties: School parties and coach parties welcome by arrangement.

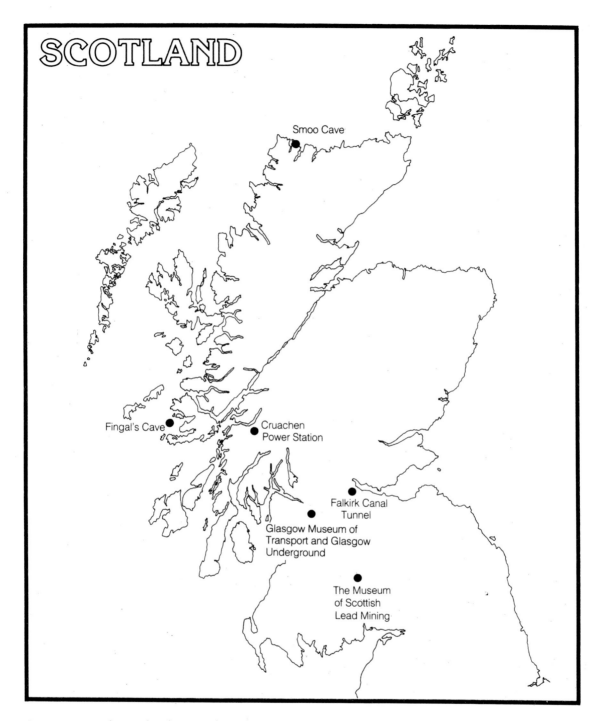

SCOTLAND

Smoo Cave

Fingal's Cave

Cruachen
Power Station

Falkirk Canal
Tunnel

Glasgow Museum of
Transport and Glasgow
Underground

The Museum
of Scottish
Lead Mining

Once you reach Scotland, everything becomes more spread out, the population more sparse and the roads quieter. Sea caves are a common sight on many parts of the coast, but if Smoo Cave is on your short list, be prepared for the majority of the roads north of Lairg to be single track with passing spaces. Do not let that put you off as the scenery more than makes up for the inconvenience. One word of caution though, look out for the fish lorries from the beautiful little port of Kinlochbervie. The drivers have a job to do and being held up by visitors trying to spot golden eagles from the middle of the A838 is not something they allow for in their schedule. By far the most awkward location to reach, unless you have ambitions to visit Maes Howe, the fine passage grave on Orkney, is Staffa. An uninhabited island off the west coast of Mull, famous for its basaltic formations and remarkable caves, of which the most famous is Fingal's Cave, the inhospitable Staffa is not a port of call on any of the regular cruise ships and ferries plying the Clyde and Hebrides. There are, however, boat trips from Oban and Iona which do land there, weather permitting, allowing time for the visitor to explore the cave immortalized by Mendelssohn.

Both the Museum of Scottish Lead Mining at Wanlockhead in the south and the gentle giant of a power station buried deep under Ben Cruachen much further north, are quite easy to reach and very well worth the effort. The electric bus ride to the heart of the mountain is an experience not to be missed. The same could well be said for the Wanlockhead Museum. There is nowhere else quite like it in the British Isles; here was hard rock mining in the raw if ever there was. In comparison the sleepy tranquility of the Edinburgh and Glasgow Union Canal at Falkirk comes as a complete contrast. It is incredible to think that before the coming of the railways linking Scotland's two main cities, clumping great horses used to thunder up and down the tow-path hauling passenger boats at a slow canter between those two cities.

It was impossible to leave Scotland without mentioning the spectacular Glasgow Museum of Transport and the new 'Clockwork Orange' which has replaced the old Victorian subway, one of the oldest true 'tube' railways in the world. You can still get a pretty good impression of what the original installation must have been like to ride on in the industrious thirties, when the great 'Queen-liners', *Mary* and *Elizabeth* were being built at John Brown's famous Clydeside yard.

Cruachen Power Station

The Cruachen Power Station produces around 400 megawatts or an estimated 450 million units of electricity each year and yet the only visible signs to identify its presence to the passing motorist or drifting fisherman, are the new Visitor's Centre and an administration block on the banks of Loch Awe. The secret lies at the end of a half mile (one kilometre) long access tunnel leading straight into the heart of the mountain. Here, in a vast underground generation hall, four 134,000 horsepower reversible Francis pump-turbines, each driving a 110/100 megawatt motor-generator, pump water up to a storage reservoir at off-peak, and stand-by to top up the grid at a moment's notice during the rest of the day. At that moment when the kettle goes on after your favourite television soap, or when the factory start-up surge drains available power first thing in the morning, or indeed whenever there is a peak load, the system automatically senses a deficiency and the machinery throbs into action. With the system fully synchronized the station can reach full load within 60 seconds. It effectively obviates the age-old inefficiency of running steam plant at part-load.

Visitors are welcomed at the well-laid-out Visitor Centre beside the Loch. It is well worth spending a short while strolling around the informative exhibition area. Colourful mimic diagrams and a video clearly describe the basic operation of the station and the enormous feat of civil engineering involved in building the dam and excavating the machinery hall and thousands of metres of tunnel. From here, assuming one has arrived early to avoid a lengthy wait, an electric mini-bus takes the visitor into the legendary Ben Cruachen itself and the visitors' gallery of the echoey 100 yard (91 metres) by 40 yard (36 metres) underground generation hall, 1,200 feet (365 metres) below the Cruachen Reservoir. Beside the long flight of steps leading up to the gallery, plants photo-synthesize quite adequately, bathed in the life-giving rays of electric lamps.

The scale is monumental, even the access tunnel looks wide enough to take a tank transporter, and yet the entire Wellsianesque complex can be controlled by a staff of three from an operations centre overlooking the machine hall. From here communication is maintained with other local hydro-electric power stations which together form the Awe Scheme.

General Information

Owner: North of Scotland Hydro-Electric Board
Title: Cruachen Power Station
Location: Dalmally, Argyll. Map reference OS sheet 50 078268
Enquiries: Visitor Centre, Cruachen Power Station
Telephone: 08662 673
Directions: On the banks of Loch Awe on the A85 Crianlarich to Oban road 5.6 miles (9 kilometres) west of Dalmally.
Access: Open daily, March to October 9 a.m.–4.30 p.m.
Nearest car park: Free car/coach parking on site
Distance: 22 yards (20 metres)
Time to explore: 45 minutes; guided tour 25 minutes
Conditions: Transport is provided to and from the underground complex. Protective clothing is not required. There is a certain amount of machinery noise. Only 25 visitors are permitted underground at any one time so arrive early to avoid delay at busy periods.
Facilities: Visitor Centre with information desk; snack bar; lavatories; waiting area. The facilities are not suitable for the disabled. Display showing stages of construction and mimic panel of operating principles. Exhibition of wind energy throughout the world. Cinema showing video film of the project.
Parties: School and coach parties welcome.

Falkirk Canal Tunnel

Canals predated other forms of transport by a sufficiently long interval for them to have become established features of the landscape before they became quaint anachronisms for sedentary anglers and supermarket trolleys. But along came the railways and better roads and the most efficient, albeit leisurely, form of transportation known to man was permitted to silt-up and decay. But, happily, there are stretches of British waterway which have been maintained and which, if we ever ceased to be able to find enough energy to send turbo-juggernauts thundering down our highways and byways, could at a pinch come in handy.

Such picturesque notions spring to mind easily when sitting in the sun on the neatly mown sward of grass at the entrance to the Falkirk tunnel on the Edinburgh and Glasgow Union Canal. Picture the gentle, sweeping curve of the beautifully kept tow-path as it passes through a rural scene of reeds and marsh grass, ducks and swans. It is only a short stretch and it is not worth driving all the way up from Cornwall to see, but it is very pleasant. It also provides an excellent vantage point to study the panorama from Stirling and the Bridge of Allan

to the north-east, round to the Firth of Forth and Dunfermline in the east. Just before the tunnel itself the towpath broadens considerably to form an excellent picnic area. The canal is lined with wild flowers and reeds and is a popular spot for fishing and a favourite place for locals to exercise their dogs.

The Edinburgh and Glasgow Union was designed to link the Forth and Clyde Canal, opened in 1791, at Camelon near Falkirk, with Edinburgh. Completed in 1822, this splendid 30 mile (48 kilometre) long waterway was cunningly designed to operate all on one level with the exception of the 110 feet (33 metre) flight of locks at the junction with the Forth and Clyde to the south of the Union Inn at Port Downie. To term it a success would be an understatement. The volume of traffic generated between the two 'capitals', both goods and passenger, exceeded the wildest dreams of the project's promoters, the route enjoying considerable popularity right up until the opening of the Edinburgh and Glasgow Railway.

Perhaps because of Scotland's convoluted coastline, with its hundreds of out-lying islands, Scots were well accustomed to hopping on a boat to get to their destination. For this reason the Forth and Clyde canal barges were designed with cabins at either end equipped with fires, tables and comfy chairs, those in the bow accommodating ten ladies, those in the stern a similar number of gentlemen. But such was the demand that in 1809 the company floated a daily passenger-only service. With the added attraction of a through trip to Edinburgh, business boomed and in 1831 a sleeper service was introduced, still segregated no doubt, and the time for the 56 miles (90 kilometres) between the two main cities was cut to less than eleven hours. Ten years later the time-table included four so-called 'swift' boats a day. Resembling over-grown rowing 'eights' rather than the bluff-bowed barges we have come to know and love, these waterway expresses were each hauled by two horses. The animals must have clumped along at quite a rate of knots since, apparently, they needed to couple-up to fresh 'nags' every two miles!

From the western end of the canal, about a mile (1.5 kilometres) away from the 696 yard (21 metre) long Falkirk tunnel, the tow-path can be followed, with diversions where the cut has been filled in, for virtually its full length. The tunnel itself is approached through a cutting and the tow-path, protected by iron railings surmounted by a stout timber handrail, narrows considerbly in order to enter the rather forbidding arched stone portals. Surprisingly, the roof is approximately flat and rough hewn from the virgin stone, here and there braced with brick reinforcing arches. Further down the tunnel there is the hollow sound of falling water which echoes the whole length of the place. The tow-path is cobbled and no doubt those of nervous disposition will be glad to hear that not only is there a light to be seen at the other end, but unless they believe in ghosts, the chances of meeting a two-horse-power-express travelling in the opposite direction in mid-tunnel is nowadays distinctly remote.

General Information

Owner: British Waterways
Title: Falkirk Canal Tunnel
Location: On the Edinburgh and Glasgow Union Canal, Low Park, Falkirk, Strathclyde. Map reference OS sheet 65 883790
Enquiries: Falkirk Tourist Information Office, The Steeple, High Street, Falkirk, Scotland
Telephone: 0324 20244
Directions: From the A803 Glasgow to Linlithgow road turn right at Glenfuir roundabout and proceed up Rosebank Distillery Road. Take the left turn into Windsor road, through the housing estate and turn right into Maggie Woods Loan. Low Park is 440 yards (400 metres) on the right. Follow the central footpath across the park, pass under the railway bridge. The canal embankment is at the top of a short rise. Turn left along the towpath for the tunnel west portal.
Access: Any reasonable time
Nearest car park: In Maggie Woods Loan
Distance: 875 yards (300 metres)
Time to explore: 45 minutes
Conditions: Open footpaths and canal towpath. The footpaths are easily negotiated by wheelchair.
Facilities: Grass picnic area. Panoramic views over River Forth.

Fingal's Cave

Known to the Norsemen as Staphi Ey, the island of pillars, the island of Staffa is situated to the west of the Isle of Mull off Scotland's west coast. This melancholy basalt bastion has captured the romantic imagination of generations of visitors – local and tourist alike. Fishermen are said to have named the island after an ancient and rather frightening Irish–Scots hero called Fionn mac Cumhaill, who, in his spare time when he wasn't ogreing around the Inner Hebrides, supposedly threw together the majestic columns and pavements of the Giant's Causeway in Northern Ireland, which is also formed from basalt. With a little imagination, it is possible to arrive at 'Fingal's' by way of 'fin-ma-cool's', playing a few games with the Gaelic en route. Would that it were so easy to arrive at Staffa!

Although it is possible to land and explore the island in calm weather, such a trip requires careful planning and a reasonably flexible time schedule. The western approaches of Mull are not the best place to be caught in a westerly gale. Happily, the dramatic formations are in some ways better observed from the sea where the parallel-piped columns can clearly be seen to have a slightly tipsy, seven degree inclination from the vertical, like an interlocked collection of black, angular, leaning towers of Pisa.

Basalt is, in fact, a common, dark coloured, fine-grained basic igneous rock. At both Staffa and in Ulster, however, exposure and the process of natural weathering have split the stone into hundreds and thousands of bizarre, towering, crystalline stumps and columns of polygonal section which appear almost to be man-made or even giant-made. In reality they were created quite naturally as the molten rock slowly cooled under conditions of tremendous pressure.

More reminiscent of the façade of a medieval cathedral, with its characteristic clusters of columns and even a crude pointed arch, the 76 yards (70 metres) long by 66 feet (20 metres) high Fingal's Cave has been romanticized to the point of over-kill. Its most famous visitor must of course have been the composer Mendelssohn who, in 1832, found the evocative, inspirational atmosphere of the rock prompted him to write his top-of-the-orchestral-pops Hebrides Overture. The Gaelic for Fingal's Cave is Ua Bhin, which roughly translated means 'musical cave'. Appropriately enough, in rough weather, the whole cave resounds with strange, moaning notes caused by wave pressure against an undersea air vent. The effect is similar to a form of natural horn and local boatmen maintain that in really bad weather, the din reaches quite frightening proportions, being audible for several miles out to sea and loud enough to be practically deafening at close quarters. In the past this has understandably given rise to some bizarre myths and legends, but in reality all it signifies is merely that Fingal's Cave is blowing its own trumpet.

General Information

Owner: The National Trust
Title: Fingal's Cave
Location: Isle of Staffa, West of Mull. Map reference OS sheet 47 325351
Enquiries: Oban Tourist Information Office, Boswell House, Argyle Square, Oban, Argyle or The National Trust, Hutchinson's Hall, 158 Ingram Street, Glasgow
Telephone: 0631 63122 or 041 552 8391
Directions: Staffa can only be reached by boat. Excursions operated by Caledonian MacBraine and Gordon Grant Tours.
Access: Any reasonable time weather permitting
Nearest car park: Oban or Fionnphort, Mull
Distance: Day trip from Oban
Conditions: Sea cave on wild, rocky island
Facilities: None. Interesting scenic tour from Oban via Isle of Mull, Staffa and Iona.
Parties: By prior arrangement with tour operators.

Glasgow Museum of Transport and Glasgow Underground

Opened to the public on 14th December 1896, about ten years from its original inception, the Glasgow District Subway, as it was then called, consisted of two parallel 4 feet (1.2 metre) gauge tracks which circumnavigated the city carrying cable-drawn cars through separate 11 feet (3.35 metres) diameter tunnels 6.5 miles (10.5 kilometres) in length. Outer circle cars ran clockwise, inner circle anti-clockwise and there were fifteen stations. But, initially, all did not go smoothly: there were teething troubles with the haulage system. Even when these had been sorted out, it was found that the average life of the 57 ton (58 tonne) cables was a mere seven and a half months. Disaster struck the system on the first day of opening, with a crash on the inner circle and a derailment on the outer. It closed and did not reopen until the following January. Despite this setback the cable-hauled system was very effective; the ubiquitous Glasgow trams were electrified from 1898 but the underground was only converted to electricity in 1935. Surprisingly, the small Victorian cars, now powered by electric motors, were retained. Fine examples of them can be found in the Glasgow Museum of Transport.

The subway has lived through very mixed

Continued overleaf

fortunes. Various economic pressures forced a major reconstruction in the 1970s. The old subway has passed into history and been replaced and updated to suit the present-day needs of its passengers. On 1st November 1979 the new system was officially opened. Bright, clean and somewhat smaller in scale than their London Underground counterparts, the brightly coloured trains come and go with a regular high-pitched rumble and hiss and so popular is this new system that it has been affectionately, albeit unofficially, named the 'clockwork orange'.

The Subway Gallery at the Museum of Transport is an accurate reconstruction of the original Merkland Street subway station. But down below, do the old platforms and passages remain? Many of the original fixtures and fittings removed from the station in 1977 have survived, giving the whole exhibit a very authentic atmosphere. All it needs to be real is the rattle of the approaching cars and the chatter of the passengers. The equipment on display includes samples of rails with clips and cable gripper, the original destination board gantry, complete with clock, and at the end of the platform, the station master's cabin with its signalling equipment, warning klaxon and lights used to indicate the approach of a train. The trailer car no. 39 is now fully restored and is truly magnificent with its beautiful wooden interior, end platforms and folding steel lattice doors. Car no. 1 was originally a 'gripper' car, and electrified, was still in use right up to the old subway closure in 1977.

General Information

Owner: Glasgow Museums and Art Galleries
Title: Glasgow Museum of Transport – Reconstruction of Merkland Street Station
Location: Albert Drive, Glasgow
Enquiries: The Keeper, The Museum of Transport, Albert Drive, Glasgow
Telephone: 041 357 3929
Directions: By Underground to Kelvinhall Bridge Station and follow signposts to the museum.
Access: Open daily, Monday to Saturday, 10 a.m.–5 p.m., Sundays 2 p.m.–5 p.m., except Christmas Day.
Nearest car park: Ample car/coach parking on site
Distance: 55 yards (50 metres)
Time to explore: Two hours minimum
Conditions: Modern air-conditioned museum building.
Facilities: Café; gift shop selling a wide range of books and souvenirs; lavatories including facilities for handicaped persons. Full facilities for the disabled. Reconstruction of Merkland Street Station.
Parties: School and coach parties welcome.

The Museum of Scottish Lead Mining

At an altitude of some 1,400 feet (427 metres) Wanlockhead is one of the highest villages in Scotland. Set in splendid isolation, high in the heather-covered slopes of the Lowther Hills, it was a centre for local lead mining until about 1950. Galena had probably been mined in the area in Roman times and from the late seventeenth century the mining of lead ore had become the main preoccupation. In 1710 a lease was taken by a group of wealthy merchants, calling themselves 'The Quaker Company', to explore and develop the mineral rights of the area. Various other companies also took an interest, taking out small leases, and soon the barren hills began to take on the typical appearance of a mining area with scars, trackways and spoil-heaps.

In 1756 the lease for the whole area was taken by Ronald Crawford, who changed the name to 'The Wanlockhead Mining Company'. For almost a century the mines prospered until the Free Trade Policy in 1832 resulted in the import of cheap lead from the Continent. When the Company's lease expired the Duke of Buccleuch took over operations. It was under his direction that the site of the smelting operations moved to Wanlock Burn. In the early part of this century the mines were re-leased to the 'Wanlockhead Lead Mining Company' who rebuilt the smelt mill and put in new machinery above and below ground. But the high cost of pumping from veins 490 feet (150 metres) below sea level and the low price of lead during the period of economic depression that followed the 1914–18 war, led to the mine closing in the 1930s. There was a brief renaissance in 1951, but this came to naught. Surveys indicate that large reserves of lead and zinc and other ores remain, but as there are cheaper sources abroad these are unlikely to be extracted in the foreseeable future. Interestingly enough the Scottish Crown jewels were made from gold and silver mined in the area.

Wanlockhead never saw the kind of rollicking prosperity enjoyed by mines like Camborne's Dolcoath or Tavistock's Devon Great Consuls. Due to the altitude, isolation and poor access, lack of fresh food and bad hygiene, it was not a happy place for the miners. A perennial problem was the type of rock in which the ore veins were found. Known by the delightful, onomatopoeic name of 'greywhacky' – actually spelt greywacke – it was far from a delightful material to extract, being cold, hard and treacherous. In the early 1700s men working rota-shifts twenty-four hours a day for a full sixty hours, using only hand-tools, no gunpowder, sometimes only moved ahead as little as an inch a day. To drive one particular level half a mile (0.8 kilometres), took eighty years.

Miners were paid about £10 to £13 a year for tunnelling, £20 a year when they hit a commercial vein. In comparison a farm worker grossed only £5. For this privilege, the miner was tied to his employment by a cunning payment system based on a 'subsist'. Paid once a year with no money in between except the subsist, out of his wages he had to pay about £13 for gun-powder, candles and tools alone, to say nothing of food and essentials, all bought, of course, from the Mining Company Store. This practice frequently resulted in a miner living and dying in debt, unable to raise the money to leave either the mine or the area. At least the farm labourer was working out in the open.

Not that the company was without its problems. The Duke took one bar of lead in every six, as his cut for being the titled landowner – a taxing task if ever there was one. Because of the tough rock no one wanted to spend money on trivial things like ventilation. In some sections men could only work half-time, on half pay naturally, as the 'air' was so bad. Pneumonia, silicosis, scurvy and lead-poisoning filled the graveyards more efficiently than old age ever did. And yet John Taylor lived to be 137 years of age, according to the Leadhills Library, incidentally also the oldest subscription library in Great Britain. Perhaps he knew something the others did not know.

The final closure of the mine spelt doom for a whole community virtually dependent on mining for its existence. The situation was so serious that there was even a threat of a Closing Order being served on the whole village. This would effectively have made Wanlockhead into a 'ghost town'. But the village was not prepared to die and at last is beginning to thrive again after a period of severe hardship. One of the main reasons for its survival is the success of the Museum of Scottish Lead Mining. Wanlockhead has become a kind of mining cottage tourist industry – paradoxically as dependant on the mine for survival as it ever was, but now the mine brings in tourists instead of taking out lead.

Stretching the entire length of the valley a clearly marked Mining Trail follows an ambling path which links library, visitor centre, church, smelt mills, Glencrieff Mine and Bay Mine. Punctuating the route is Williamson's Drift – the section of mine which is open to the public, a unique nineteenth-century water-powered wooden beam pumping engine and the charming Museum Cottages, where the visitor can see the home comforts of the people who once populated this quaint and somehow curiously endearing village. Part candle-lit, the cottage interiors have a 'presence' that makes them perhaps the most authenic of their kind to be seen in the British Isles. Try to get to Wanlockhead, it is not all that far off the beaten track nowadays and it is rather special.

General Information

Owner: Wanlockhead Museum Trust
Title: The Museum of Scottish Lead Mining
Location: Goldscaur Row, Wanlockhead, Strathclyde. Map reference OS sheet 78 871131
Enquiries: The Museum of Scottish Lead Mining
Telephone: 0659 74387
Directions: Proceed north on the A74 Carlisle to Glasgow road from Beattock. Take the A791 signposted to Elvanfoot. After

Continued overleaf

one mile (1.5 kilometres) turn right along the B7040. After a further 6 miles (10 kilometres) take the B797 and proceed to Wanlockhead.
Access: Open daily, Easter to September 11 a.m.–4.30 p.m. Last underground tour 3.30 p.m.
Nearest car park: Ample free car/coach parking at the museum
Distance: 110 yards (100 metres)
Time to explore: Three hours minimum. Guided tour half an hour.
Conditions: Generally dry graded footpaths throughout. The roof is low in places. Stout footwear is recommended. Protective headgear is provided free.
Facilities: Museum; gift shop selling a range of books, souvenirs and the famous Sanquhar knitwear; picnic area; lavatories. The facilities are suitable for the more adventurous disabled. There is an impressive collection of lead-mining artefacts on display at the museum. The surrounding countryside offers superb scope for the walker.
Parties: School parties and coach parties welcome but please book in advance.

Smoo Cave

Whilst there are any number of sea caves to be seen around the coast of Scotland, few are as accessible or as spectacular as Smoo Cave, which more than justifies a visit. Situated at Leirinmore, 1 mile (1.6 kilometres) east of Durness, this spectacular sea cave should not be missed by anyone visiting the far north of Scotland. Stretching back over 200 feet (60 metres) from the cliff face, with its 110 feet (34 metres) wide, 60 feet (18 metres) high maw gaping out to sea, this cave is one of the most awe inspiring sights and sounds to be found on mainland Britain.

The cave itself is reached from the car park at Leirinmore by an easy footpath, and a short scramble over the rocks. On superficial inspection, it would be logical to assume that it has been formed entirely by the action of wind and tide, were it not for the presence of two small streams which converge in the main chamber, suggesting that the cave may well owe its origins as much to fresh water as to salt. The left hand stream emerges from the base of a mass of flowstone behind which there is only a small blind chamber. The one on the right, however, is of more interest. It flows from under a natural rock bridge beyond which there is a further large chamber. This contains an underground lake fed by the Allt Smoo, a moorland burn which tumbles about 80 feet (24 metres) down an almost vertical shaft, filling the echoing interior of the cave with the sounds of falling water. The roof of the cave is punctuated by a series of blow-holes formed many centuries ago, presumably before the cave ceased to be tidal, by the natural action of the sea forcing its way through fissures in the roof.

General Information

Owner: Highland Regional Council
Title: Smoo Cave
Location: Durness, North Scottish Highland Region. Map reference OS sheet 9 419679
Enquiries: Durness Information Centre, Durness, By Lairg or Highland Regional Council, Glen Urquehart Road, Inverness
Telephone: 097181 259 or 0463 234121
Directions: One mile (1.6 kilometres) east of Durness on A838 to Leirinmore.
Access: Any reasonable time
Nearest car park: Ample free car/coach parking near site.
Distance: Short walk down to cave
Time to explore: 45 minutes
Conditions: Sea cave
Facilities: None.

BIBLIOGRAPHY

A Child's War – The German Occupation of Guernsey as seen through young eyes . . ., Molly Bihet, Molley Bihet, St Peter Port, Guernsey, 1985

A History of Lead Mining in the Pennines, Raistrick, Arthur and Jennings, Longman, 1965

Archeology of Canals, P J G Ransom, Worlds Work, 1979

British Railway History, Hamilton Ellis, Allen & Unwin, 1959

Archeology of Railways, P J G Ransom, Worlds Work, 1981

Caves of Derbyshire, Trevor Ford, Dalesman, 1974

CEGB Year Book, 1987

Civil Engineering – Railways, B Morgan, Longman, 1971

Coniston Copper Mines: A Field Guide, Eric Holland, Cicerone Press, 1986

Creswell Crags Seminar January 1986 PD1554, Report of the Creswell Crags Seminar 15–16 January 1986

Creswell Crags: Late Pleistocene Sites in the East Midlands, British Archeological Reports – Easter 1984

Landscape and Antiquity, Kenneth Woodbridge, Oxford, 1970

Lead Mining in the Peak District, compiled by members of the Peak District Mines Historical Society, edited by Trevor D Ford and J H Rieuwerts, Peak Park Joint Planning Board, 1983

Lost Canals and Waterways of Britain, Ronald Russell, David & Charles, 1982

Navigable Waterways, L T C Rolt, Longman, 1969

Studies in Speleology Vol 1, Wendy Davies, The Willian Pengelly Cave Studies Association, 1964

The Dashwoods of West Wycombe, Sir Francis Dashwood, Aurum Press, 1987

The Encyclopaedia of Geomorphology, Rhodes W Fairbridge, Reinhold Books Corp., 1968

The Genius of the Place, Hunt and Willis, Paul Elek, 1975

The Hell-Fire Club, Donald McCormick, Jarrolds, 1958

The Limestone and Caves of Northwest England, A C Waltham, David and Charles, 1974

The Natural Wonders of the British Isles, Charles Walker, Book Club Associates – Orbis Publishing Ltd, 1982

The War in the Channel Islands – Then and Now, Winston G Ramsay, Battle of Britain Prints International Ltd, 1981

Underground Britain, A Guide to the Wild Caves and Show Caves of England, Scotland and Wales, Bruce Bedford, Willow Books – Collins, 1985

Underground Railways of the World, H P C Havers, Temple Press, 1966

USEFUL ADDRESSES

British Cave Research Association, Bethel Green, Calderbrook Road, Littleborough, Lancashire

Derbyshire Caving Association, c/o Sports Council, 26 Musters Road, Westbridgeford, Nottinghamshire

National Caving Association, c/o Dr Warwick, Geography Department, University of Birmingham, Edgebaston, Birmingham 15

Eldon Pothole Club, c/o D W Gill, 54 Lr Lane, Chinley, Stockport Cheshire. Tel: 0663 50487

Peak District Mines Historical Society, 12 Rowley Gardens, Littleover, Derbyshire

Peakland Archeological Society, c/o The Crescent, Hayfield Road, Chapel-en-le-Frith, Derbyshire

GLOSSARY

Adit: a horizontal tunnel into a mine from a hillside, often called a level, through which the mine is drained and ventilated.

Adventurers: mine shareholders or speculators.

Bellpit: a shallow mine shaft which flares out below ground like a bell.

Barytes: barium sulphate

Blende: zinc sulphide

Blue John: banded blue and white fluorspar found only at Treak Cliff, Castleton.

Calcite: calcium carbonate

Cassiterite: tin oxide, a common ore of tin.

Chalcopypite: copper-iron-sulphide, a common ore of copper.

Count house: a mine office, often where ore was weighed and assayed.

Coffin level: a horizontal tunnel shaped like a coffin.

Crawl: an extremely low narrow section in a natural cave or pot hole.

Deads: waste, non-orebearing material left below ground in a mine.

Diagenesis: the physical, chemical and biological changes that take place in sediments before they become consolidated or the formation of larger crystals from smaller ones.

Dog's leg tunnel: a mine level in which straight sections are combined with sharp bends.

Dressing floor: the floor where ore is broken down into small particles prior to treatment to extract the metal.

Dressing mill: a mill for breaking rough ore into fine particles for further treatment.

Drift: a tunnel or level.

Fluorspar: the mineral fluorite, calcium fluoride.

Feldspar or **felspar:** a group of crystalline minerals consisting of aluminium silicates containing either potassium, sodium, calcium or barium.

Flowstone: strictly any formation produced by the evaporation of waters which have passed through limestone and thus contain calcium carbonate in solution (see stalactites and stalagmites).

Fogou: the name given to the curious tunnels found in late Iron Age settlements. The term is derived from an old Cornish word for cave.

Galena: the mineral lead sulphide, the chief ore of lead.

Gin circle: a circular ore-crusher, usually horse-drawn, sometimes called a horse gin.

Gour pools: also known as rimstone pools, they are formed when groundwater is ponded by irregularities on a flowstone floor causing preferential rim deposits which become self-perpetuating, forming a series of stepped pools.

Heading: the development end of a mine level.

Inclusion: a gaseous, liquid or solid substance enclosed in a mineral mass.

Kibble: a large, usually iron bucket used to raise ore up a mine shaft.

Lode: a mineral bearing vein.

Old man: miners' term for old workings or to describe miners of long ago.

Pitch: a steep vertical drop in a natural or wild cave.

Pot hole: strictly a circular hole formed in the rocky bed of a river or water course by the grinding action of stones or gravel whirled down by the water. Any extended underground system of caverns or passages formed by the action of water.

Revetment: a stone-faced retaining wall supporting an embankment.

Siphon: a flooded section of a cave or pot hole linking two non-flooded sections, where the roof descends below the water level.

Sough: an adit or tunnel driven specifically to drain a mine.

Souterrain: an underground chamber, store room or passage.

Stemple: a piece of wood wedged across a working or vein for use as a climbing way or the support for a platform or roof.

Stope: a worked out vein left as an open cavity, it may be only inches wide or enormous.

Spoil: waste material from mining operations.

Stamps: machines for crushing ore using heavy baulks of timber shod with iron 'heads' lifted by mechanical means, a battery of such machines.

Vein: a body of minerals enclosed by rock.

Wheel pit: the pit housing a large water-wheel.

Whim: a winding engine or winch worked by horse or steam power.

Wild cave: a natural cave or pot hole which has not been made 'safe', i.e. paved, fitted with electric light, safety rails, etc. and from which such features as crawls, pitches and siphons have not been bypassed.

Winze: a small shaft inside a mine, i.e. a shaft that does not go to the surface.

INDEX OF ENTRIES

Wales

Scotland